GADGETS & GAMES
FROM THE 1950S
TO THE 1990S

GADGETS & GAMES FROM THE 1950S TO THE 1990S

Daniel Blythe

First published in Great Britain in 2011 by
Remember When
an imprint of
Pen & Sword Books Ltd
47 Church Street
Barnsley
South Yorkshire
S70 2AS

ISBN: 978-1-84468-105-1

Typeset in 11/13pt Palatino by
Concept, Huddersfield, West Yorkshire

Printed and bound by
Replika Press Pvt. Ltd.

Pen & Sword Books Ltd incorporates the Imprints of Pen & Sword
Aviation, Pen & Sword Family History, Pen & Sword Maritime, Pen &
Sword Military, Pen & Sword Discovery, Wharncliffe Local History,
Wharncliffe True Crime, Wharncliffe Transport, Pen & Sword Select, Pen &
Sword Military Classics, Leo Cooper, The Praetorian Press, Remember
When, Seaforth Publishing and Frontline Publishing.

For a complete list of Pen & Sword titles please contact
PEN & SWORD BOOKS LIMITED
47 Church Street, Barnsley, South Yorkshire, S70 2AS, England
E-mail: enquiries@pen-and-sword.co.uk
Website: www.pen-and-sword.co.uk

Contents

Introduction

What enabled Homo sapiens to become the dominant species on Earth? Many experts say it's our wonderful brains, whose complexity could not be reproduced without building a computer the size of Tokyo. Some say it's our resourcefulness, our indomitable nature, our ability to bounce back from every disaster. And some would suggest it's our innate ability to exterminate the competition.

But some have argued that it's much simpler than that. Perhaps our possession of the opposable thumb is that key biological trait – the talent which enables us to be tool-makers. From the first Bronze Age axe-wielders to the armourers and blacksmiths of the Middle Ages and the jewellers, microsurgeons, plumbers and programmers of today, we use our hands to do and make things. And that's the human race all over, if you think about it. We create. We make things. We make what you might call *stuff*. We leave objects for posterity.

Sometimes, we make too many things and are not sure where we ought to leave them all. To attempt to climb Everest was a brave and noble idea back in 1953, but you rather feel that if a time-traveller from 50 years in the future had shown Sir Edmund Hillary a picture of the landfill site it was to become, he might not have bothered. Human history might well have turned out very differently – maybe we'd have given up on the idea of mountain climbing, and never even continued the long look upwards which got us on the moon 16 years later.

Someone who was born just before Neil Armstrong's giant leap can often find the plethora of objects with which the world is cluttered vastly bewildering. But this is how, as humans, we make our mark on the world: it's almost as if something isn't really there unless we have built something on it, made something out of it, taken a photograph of it or stuffed it and served it up on a platter with a lemon in its mouth. Or sometimes all four. Our legacy to the world, when the human race is finally extinguished, will be all our things, our objects. Everything from the wheel and the axe to the technology which has brought us broadband internet, wi-fi and instant sushi bars. We make the culture we live in; we *manufacture* our environment like no other creature on the planet.

But it's amazing how quickly our creations become obsolete. If you look at a wedding photograph from 1975, it won't be the trees or the sky which help you to pin the date down, it'll be the bloke with the Noddy Holder sideburns and kipper tie, or the woman with the Yoko parting, hideous floral print dress and huge glasses. Plus, of course, the waiting car, which will look like a chunky, industrial museum-piece. Look at the mid-eighties: MTV is a shiny new idea, as is the ability to record a TV programme and watch it later. It's less than a generation, too, since inventor Sir Clive Sinclair chugged along in his C5 (and was, for a few weeks, taken seriously as a saviour from traffic congestion). And if you travel back in time to somewhere even as recent as the mid-nineties, you'll be shocked: all those students with their Jarvis Cocker haircuts and Blur T-shirts, using their wheezing Word for Windows 2.0 to write essays, using clunky old Telnet for their Internet access and *not* walking around with mobile phones.

The landscape changes imperceptibly as we make new objects and our old ones fall into disuse. The red telephone box, for example, used to be as much a part of a village green as a pub, a pump and a maypole. For a while, those clear plastic booths started to replace them, to the horror of preservation societies across the land. And now, the red phone box is a relic. First the Police Box slipped quietly into obscurity as police acquired hand-held radios. And now the telephone box too has dematerialised, as it sadly can't compete with the little space-age silver boxes which can send digital pictures, play miniature versions of Space Invaders and assault the ears of fellow passengers with a rendition of the Crazy Frog ringtone.

There are many things the human race has made which are just too new to be put into a glass case and admired, and yet are too old to be used any more. If you are a youngish or middle-aged adult today, the chances are that you were, at some point, fascinated by the process of making an instant Vesta Curry, or taking a photograph with a Polaroid and watching the ghosts slowly resolve themselves into blue-tinged images of your friends and family. You may have wondered how on earth to get out of the Goblins' Dungeon in the computer adventure game Hobbit, or buzzed around a virtual maze eating the Pac-Man pills. The Rubik Cube kept an entire generation in thrall, until someone found and published the solution – these days, the code would be on a website before the toy was even on sale. Perhaps you watched the first-ever Space Shuttle launch on a tiny portable television, or listened to your first C60 tape compilation on an early Sony Walkman with bright red headphones. You may even have been skateboarding as you did so. Perhaps, like Jason Donovan in *Neighbours*, you skateboarded down the hill to work while wooing the local bubble-permed sex goddess. Perhaps not.

We entertained ourselves in ways which seemed sophisticated at the time – the 'white heat of technology' gave way to the soft green glow of the electronic age. Children hunched over the all-knowing Simon toy, ready to reproduce the ever-more-complex melodies which he threw at them. The power of a tape-to-tape sound system meant that you could record your friend's copy of *Now 3* for your own listening. And can there be any former schoolchild alive who didn't put the number 5318008 into a pocket calculator, then turn it upside-down to giggle insanely at the result?

We now live among a generation who find cassette tapes to be a curio, items of nostalgia value which one might see on *Ashes To Ashes* or *Life On Mars*. Like jukeboxes, they and the machines that played them are now quaint, associated with the music of a particular era. So how long before the mp3 player goes the same way? As the music industry strives to produce sound which is bigger, better, sharper, clearer, are we losing the organic, raw feel of the old vinyl records? And just what will remain, in 20 years' time, to play your double cassette version of *Now 47*?

Furthermore. . .

It is the now-traditional battle-cry of the parent that kids didn't do things like that in their day. If you believe what you hear, there's no way we were hunched over our Commodore 64 or ZX Spectrum keyboards, moving jagged shapes around on flickering TV screens. No, we were out in the fresh, oxygen-rich country air, manfully smiting hedges with a switch, fording dams and constructing elaborate dens, or climbing trees with aplomb to survey the countryside, and we would return, muddy, trousers ripped, but with cheeks glowing with ruddy health, ready for a bath and a tea of hearty sandwiches and buns. Or, if it was raining, we were playing games. 'Proper' games. It's amazing how the memory is able to associate disproportionate amounts of childhood with these somehow character-building, table-top activities. Occasionally, the fortysomething dad will get a glint in his eye and decide that his children need to be taught the value of money by acquiring property in Monopoly, or to learn Edifying Vocabulary through competitive three-hour stints of Scrabble. He soon regrets it when his children learn how to make the best use of a Z on Triple Word Score and have him scuttling to the dictionary – or to acquire three hotels on Mayfair and thus, virtually replicate what they have already been doing in real life and clean his wallet out.

Besides, if it's true that people's youthful gaming experiences form their characters as adults, then those PacMan fans who entered maturity in the 1990s would have had a strange predilection for drifting around darkened, labyrinthine rooms, being chased by spectral shapes, and guzzling weird pills to the sound of discordantly bleeping electronic music. And of course, that never happened…

So here, in the form of things we have made, is an exhibition of the human race's unique instinct for self-preservation. Here are our graven images and our vanished monuments – our toy, game and gadget creations.

Travel back in time with this book, your friendly guide to icons of gaming and gadgetry of the past – and gaze in wonder on the variety, the beauty and the sheer folly of our works.

Chapter 1

(There's) Always Something There To Remind Me

Top Fifties & Sixties Gadgets

- **The TV Remote Control:** Yes, it's a product of the 1950s, however much we may associate it with 1980s videos and the image of Homer Simpson sprawled in his armchair knocking back a can of Duff beer. No longer would you have to rouse yourself from your sedentary position to switch between the two available channels. The 'Lazy Bones' remote was connected by a wire to the TV, but the first ever wireless remote-control was designed by Eugene Polley and known as the 'Flash-matic' – it operated by means of light aimed at photo-cells. Ultrasonic units took over from 1956 until 1982, when infra-red became the norm
- **The Microwave Oven:** Percy Spencer, working on active radar sets for defence contractor Raytheon, noticed that a candy-bar in his pocket had started to melt – and saw the application. The patent was filed in 1945, and by the 1950s the Tappan Stove Company introduced the first home microwave oven
- **The Cordless Drill:** The first Black and Decker cordless drill was brought out in 1961, but it wasn't terribly powerful – only the arrival of nickel-cadmium batteries 20 years later made it a viable proposition at last
- **The computer mouse:** The first prototype was invented by Douglas Engelbart and Bill English in 1963 at the Stanford Research Institute
- **The Moog Synthesiser:** Robert Moog's revolutionary analogue sound-manipulator came out in 1964, just a year after BBC Radiophonic Workshop sorceress Delia Derbyshire had worked her magic on the *Doctor Who* theme tune with old-fashioned tape-splicing methods. The 1967 Monterey Pop festival helped to raise the profile of what would arguably be the most defining and revolutionary instrument of the next 25 years in popular music. A 1960s Moog can sell for over £1,500 in good condition

- **The Arpanet:** The connection of four separate computers in 1969, which would eventually lead to the Internet revolution of the 1990s and 2000s

Monopoly

The essential: Capitalism for beginners

The empire began: 1934

Current value: Brand new sets for around £13, £40 for a 'nostalgia edition' reproducing the look of the 1930s game. Vintage 1970s editions can be found in reasonable condition for under £6. The Landlord's Game, the forerunner of Monopoly, can sell for £10,000+

Whether you see it as an essential primer in city geography and relative property values, an introduction to a capitalist economy or a way of making a long Sunday afternoon go by more quickly – or, indeed, tiresomely tedious – there is no doubting Monopoly's dominance of the board game arena. Cited by many sources as the best-selling board game ever (the game has sold over 250 million sets worldwide), its appeal lies in its essential simplicity coupled with its versatility, and its ability to produce long, involved, cut-throat contests and bravura displays of ruthlessness.

The game was purportedly invented by salesman Charles Darrow, but it is now accepted that his place in history should be that of one of the game's developers. It is based on The Landlord's Game patented by one Elizabeth Magie as early as 1904. Darrow obtained a copyright for the game in 1933, and this early version featured many of the icons still associated with the game today, such as the big red GO arrow.

The rules of Monopoly are very simple to grasp – essentially, players, represented by metal icons (a car, a hat, a battleship and others) are given a set amount of toy money. They then move round the board in a clockwise direction beginning (in the main UK version) in London's impoverished districts, Old Kent Road and Whitechapel, coloured mud-brown, and ending up in the leafy boulevards of Park Lane and Mayfair, coloured a rich purple, then back to the start – aiming, on the way, to buy properties, represented by cards. Each time a player gets back to the start, he or she acquires another £200 in their personal fortune. Once a player owns a property, he or she can start being a filthy capitalist landlord, ignoring brownfield site regulations and building houses and hotels on the relevant street. And woe betide any other player who lands on a built-up space – because, even though they are just visiting, they are then charged with a whacking great amount of rent.

The aim, a rather callous one in this post-credit-crunch age, is to make your opponent(s) bankrupt. Variations involving sub-prime mortgages and runs on banks have, sadly, not yet made it into the Monopoly canon.

RetroFax

- Fans of Monopoly have played the game in all sorts of weird and wonderful places – including underwater (a diving club in Buffalo, USA in 1983) and inside a lift
- The most expensive Monopoly game was made by Alfred Dunhill. It sold for $25,000 and included gold and silver houses and hotels
- The moustached, cane-wielding, top-hatted icon of the game was originally called Rich Uncle Pennybags – his name was changed to 'Mr Monopoly' in 1998
- Some of the American streets in the original Monopoly no longer exist. Illinois Avenue, for example, was renamed Martin Luther King Jr. Boulevard in the 1980s
- Believe it or not, you can also analyse your personality based on your choice of Monopoly counter. Those who favour the Car are supposedly confident and drive a hard bargain. Battleship players are aggressive and see everything as a challenge. The Dog is chosen by players of tenacity and courage. The Boot – experienced and wise. The Iron – neat, tidy and smooth. And the player who chooses the Top Hat aspires to the finer things in life. One has to ask – do people actually get *paid* to come up with this stuff?
- The shortest possible game of Monopoly (based on the US version) can last just two turns per player. It presumes a great deal of luck on one side and misfortune with the dice and the cards on the other, but it's theoretically possible to be done and dusted in half a minute
- In the 1930s, Waddingtons attempted to cash in on the success of Monopoly with a horse-racing version called Totopoly. Surviving sets can sell for £70
- A handmade Monopoly game by Charles Darrow sold for £40,218 at a US auction in 1992

See also

The Monopoly book: Strategy and tactics of the world's most popular game by Maxine Brady (David McKay Co., 1976)

http://ownthedollar.com/2010/03/top-ten-dumbest-versions-of-monopoly-board-game/ The Monopoly variations which website Own The Dollar thinks are the 'dumbest' of all time. Some of these sound great fun... not.

They Said What?
'I think it's wrong that only one company makes the game Monopoly.'
Steven Wright, comedian.

The rarer Pokémon version of *Monopoly*.

View-Master

The essential: a mini-world in visual stereo!

Viewing began: since 1939, but peak period 1950s–70s

Current value: £10–£15 for a vintage Sawyer's View-Master from the 1960s

Three-dimensional images! We may think of them now as part of a world where James Cameron's *Avatar* leaps out of a cinema screen at a crowd bedecked in glasses with red-and-blue lenses, but it's perhaps surprising to learn that the principle dates back over 70 years. And it wasn't initially designed as a toy – it was an educational device, and a means of viewing images aimed at tourists.

When Harold Graves, president of Sawyer's Photo Services (a company which had already been established for a couple of decades) met photographer William Gruber, together they came up with an idea for adapting stereoscopic imaging (invented by Sir Charles Wheatstone in 1838), which gives the illusion of depth to a 2-D image. The key new element was Kodachrome film, which had just been developed by Eastman Kodak in 1935. After being unveiled at the New York World's Fair in 1939, the View-Master was marketed as an alternative to the postcard. And soon the appeal grew. The model was refined throughout the 1950s, with the Bakelite casing being replaced with plastic in 1962. It was purchased and popularised in the 1960s by the General Aniline and Film Corporation, and the marketing became more focused on a young audience, with images featuring toys and cartoons. The device was subsequently produced by Tyco Toys and is now produced as part of Mattel's Fisher-Price range.

RetroFax

- The United States military found the View-Master very useful, and commissioned viewing reels to help with aircraft identification
- View-Master slides have been produced to tie in with many TV shows and films, such as *Jurassic Park* and *Doctor Who*. Among the rarest are sets based around the 1966 TV show *The Munsters*, worth £60–£70, and 1967's *Lost in Space*, worth £40–£50
- View-Master features in America's National Toy Hall of Fame, which honours toys with longevity

See also

http://www.museumofplay.org/NTHoF/index.php for the National Toy Hall of Fame

http://www.vmresource.com/scenic.htm for some popular scenic reels

http://www.berezin.com/3d/Viewmaster_guide.htm for a comprehensive guide to View-Master pricing (website contains some PDFs of the book)

http://carrotrevolution.blogspot.com/2008/11/view-master.html to see a clever construction – View-Master and digital graphics combined to make a 3-D Flintstones image

The View-Master in all its glory.

Slinky

The essential: Stair-climbing spring

Slunk into view: 1945

Current value: Most collectable version is the *Toy Story* Slinky Dog, which can fetch over £40 in excellent condition and boxed. A standard pre-1990s Slinky is hard to find; imitations such as the Magic Spring abound

Another of those toys which have been around for longer than you might think, and whose essential simplicity is its key feature. Invented in wartime by naval engineer Richard James, the Slinky is a helical spring designed to work with gravity which, in a rather beautiful way, can appear to move and re-form itself as it unfurls and descends a flight of stairs with alarming precision. James was apparently inspired by the way a torsion spring fell off a ship's deck and flipped over.

Despite the Slinky being developed in the middle of the Second World War – when one would have thought the need for steel wire was rather pressing elsewhere – military applications were not immediately apparent. However, the US Army apparently used them as radio antennae in the Vietnam War.

RetroFax
- When first unveiled at Gimbel's department store in Philadelphia, USA, Slinky sold out of its entire stock of 400 in just over an hour
- Slinky is made of 80 feet of compressed steel wire, wound into 98 coils
- Richard James departed for Bolivia to work for a religious group in the early 1960s, and died in 1974

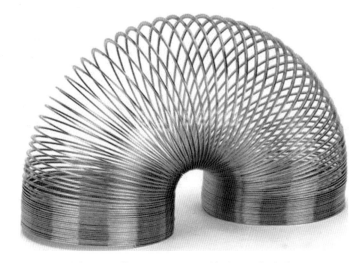

The metallic masterpiece: Slinky unfurled.

- The toy declined in popularity at the start of the 1960s, but has had resurgences since
- In 1985, the Slinky was one of several toys whose behaviour in weightless conditions was studied by the crew of the *Discovery* shuttle. Astronaut Dr Margaret Rhea Seddon reported that the Slinky lost its 'slinkiness' and instead 'sort of drooped'
- Slinky was named by Betty James, toymaker and Richard's wife, who decided that the word best described the sound of the spring unfurling. Betty James died at the age of 90 in 2008
- In the 1990s, the Slinky Dog gave the toy another lease of life, its popularity boosted further by the film *Toy Story*. By this time over 200 million Slinkys had been made and distributed worldwide

---

They Said What?
'So many children can't have expensive toys, and I feel a real obligation to them. I'm appalled when I go Christmas shopping and $60 to $80 for a toy is nothing. With 16 grandchildren you can go into the national debt.' Betty James in 1996, on her desire to create an affordable toy.

Scrabble

The essential: Ultimate strategic word-game

First tile played: 1948

Current value: Some vintage 1970s sets in excellent condition and boxed, upwards of £40. A battered 1950s edition can be picked up for as little as £5. The 50th anniversary edition, £35. A rarity is the red-and-gold-boxed Television Scrabble, specially produced for the contestants on the *Television Scrabble* TV show hosted by Alan Coren in the 1980s – boxed and unopened, this can be worth £35–£40

The classic word game – contributor to family education and improvement, provider of hours of lexical entertainment and vocabulary-expanding fun. Actually, who are we trying to kid? Along with Pictionary and Trivial Pursuit, Scrabble is probably a major contributor to family rows and disagreements. Stories abound of 'Scrabble moments' when Auntie Vera insisted on pluralising WHEAT, or squabbles over JOE being a proper noun, or AWOL being an acronym acceptable as a word in its own right.

The idea is very simple. Tiles marked with letters are placed on a board, crossword-style, to make words – the letters score according to how rare they are, so the various Es and Os are worth one point each while the Z, for example, nets a whole 10 points and the Holy Grail of Scrabble is to try and find a Triple Letter Score on which to put what Shakespeare called the 'unnecessary letter', especially if it can be made to work both vertically and horizontally and therefore score twice.

The game was invented by a young architect called Alfred Mosher Butts. Originally called Lexico, then Criss-Cross Words, Scrabble was conceived with the idea of combining the skills from various types of entertainment: dice-rolling games, number games, crossword puzzles and other word games, and 'move' games like chess. It incorporates elements of all of these, yet still manages to maintain its own unique character. Alfred Butts assigned values to the letters in the alphabet, and determined their availability in the box, by making a study of the front page of the *New York Times*. He didn't automatically provide more of the most popular letters, though. The S, one of the most common letters in the English language, was restricted to four tiles to make the formation of plurals more difficult. The pluralisation of a singular noun is still one of Scrabble players' most popular and cunning ways of forming a vertical word against a horizontal.

Staple of rainy days and Mondays in the decades before home computing, Scrabble has taken on a new lease of life online, proving especially popular with Facebook users. The transition wasn't easy, though, as Hasbro, owners of the trademark in the US and Canada, suppressed the use of Scrabble imitation Scrabulous, which was the first Facebook version of the game to take off – even though it was re-igniting interest in the game and helping sales.

RetroFax
- Scrabble is taken very seriously throughout the world, with an annual World Scrabble Championship held every second year since 1991. Players are not penalised for scoring with swear words and 'inappropriate' language – any word in the *Scrabble Dictionary* is allowed
- The youngest National Champion was Allan Saldanha, who was just 15 in 1993 when he won the title – a few years previously, Allan had been the youngest contestant on Channel 4's words-and-numbers game show *Countdown*
- Several attempts have been made to bring the game to the small screen, most notably the oddly slow-moving 1980s version on Channel 4, hosted by Alan Coren, and the more upbeat Challenge TV incarnation presented by Toby Anstis and Eamonn Holmes. An American TV version ran from 1984 to 1990
- Various editions of Scrabble exist throughout the world – to date, in over 30 languages. There is no X, Q or Z in the Welsh version, Scrabble yn Gymraeg, as they are not needed. However, it does have a double L and double F

Standard Scrabble board
– home of many a family
fallout...

- The Z, highest scoring letter in the English version, is worth only one point in the Polish edition... as one might expect
- ETAERIO is the seven-letter word you're most likely to get on the rack (and using all seven letters scores you a 50-point bonus or 'bingo'). It means 'an aggregate cluster of fruit derived from a single flower'
- The game, first trademarked as Scrabble in 1948, celebrated its 50th birthday in 1998 by staging the world's biggest game – literally – at Wembley Stadium, on a board measuring 900 square metres and with tiles the size of small patios
- In the United States, Scrabble is not the most popular board game of all. The joys of its weasly wordplay are still second fiddle to the capitalist cut-and-thrust of the other rainy Sunday standby, Monopoly.

See also

Official site at http://www.scrabble.com/

Tips from the experts at http://www.mattelscrabble.com/en/adults/index.html

The Association of British Scrabble Players can be found at http://www.absp.org.uk/

The Transistor Radio

The essential: Cheap and portable, the original iPod

Patent and prototype: 1948

Current value: hugely variable – see below! An original Regency model in good condition can fetch $1,000 (around £650)

Anyone studying the 1950s and looking for a symbol of that new invention, the 'teenager', could do worse than choose the transistor radio. Hip, compact and beautiful, the 1950s transistor radio sports, it has been noted, many design features in common with today's iPods – similar size, sci-fi-influenced design, portability, with the central wheel a prominent feature. Of course, in the transistor the wheel was a tuning knob, and a gateway to the many radio stations out there playing the hit songs of the day.

The first ever radios, made with valve receivers and popularised from the 1920s onwards, were seen as expensive. But transistors democratised the technology by making it cheap, just as other technical innovations have done over the years. The first commercial transistor radio appeared in 1954, six years after the patent, and it was called the Regency TR-1 – it was a collaboration between Texas Instruments, who made the prototype, and a small Indianapolis-based company called Industrial Development Engineering Associates (IDEA Corporation, later Regency Electronics) who developed and marketed it. The visionary Executive Vice-President of Texas instruments, Pat Haggerty, aimed to produce hundreds of thousands of transistor radios. The revolutionary invention was launched in New York and Los Angeles by on October 18th 1954, in time to take advantage of Christmas sales.

The height of 70s audio fashion – the tranny.

RetroFax

- Sony's first commercially-produced radio, the TR-55, arrived in 1955 but was never distributed in the United States. This model is now very rare. Sony's first radio to be distributed in the USA was the TR-63, which arrived in 1957 to great acclaim – it was considered the world's first true 'pocket radio'
- TR-63s appear often on eBay but even damaged models fetch up to $400. Obviously those in mint condition will go for even more
- Some Japanese models have beautiful three-dimensional patterns on them thanks to a technique known as reverse-painting
- 'Transistor Wars' began in the 1960s. Transistor prices had come down so much that manufacturers could increase the count of the transistors in their radios – supposedly for better performance. However, only eight transistors were actually active in most models, and so claims that the model had 16, 18 or more transistors were largely irrelevant! The extra transistors were there, but were 'dud' and just soldered in to bump up the numbers and back up the extraordinary claims
- Emerson's 888 series radios (1958–60) were among the most popular of what were known as the 'coat pocket' models. Many models were produced, named after US Space programs like Vanguard and Satellite. They are among the easiest models to find and are priced at $20 to $100 (£12 to £65) depending on condition

See also

Some real transistor-love at http://www.jamesbutters.com/

http://tabiwallah.com/radiowallah/ Many pictures of original transistor radios from the 1950s.

http://www.flickr.com/photos/transistor_radios/ for more beautiful photos of transistor radios in many colours.

http://www.collectorsweekly.com/radios/transistor for the serious collector's information.

http://people.msoe.edu/~reyer/regency/ for facts and statistics about the original marketing, and much more.

Lego

The essential: Ultimate construction kit

Off the blocks: 1949

Current value: hugely variable according to set. See below

Qualifies here thanks to its perennial appeal for all ages from toddlers to teenagers – and beyond… Lego is perhaps the ultimate toy, its versatile range of interlocking coloured bricks challenging children not just to play in a passive way with the items available but to create and diversify, to mix and match. It's the perfect toy for the little construction engineer who loves following the instructions to build a motorbike or tractor, but also ideal for the anarchic, creative child who wants to build weird and wonderful spaceships and then skim them across the kitchen floor to see if they can smash against the skirting-board. Lego can be anything and everything. It can be the building-blocks for something as simple as a wall or a house, or as complex as a motorbike or a *Star Wars* spaceship.

The genius of Lego is its combination of durability combined with its versatility. It can be played with again and again, in an endless series of combinations. Even Technical Lego sets, with their gears and pistons, could be creatively bastardised to make all manner of weird and wonderful devices which didn't appear on the instruction sheet. All its pieces are

Lego house with its box,
ready to be assembled.

compatible, no matter which set they come from – allowing for endless creative play.

The Lego group is based in Denmark, and since the 1940s their empire has spread to encompass games, video games and theme-parks. It had its humble beginnings in the carpentry workshop of one Ole Kirk Christiansen, who began making wooden toys after losing his job in the Great Depression of the 1930s. His company expanded into plastic bricks in the 1940s, and the famous interlocking bricks were first produced in 1949.

RetroFax
- The name Lego comes from the Danish *leg godt* (meaning 'play well').
- Lego pieces are manufactured from a strong, resilient plastic known as ABS, or acrylonitrile butadiene styrene
- There is a huge variety of themed Lego sets, encompassing space travel, vehicles, robots, dinosaurs, cowboys and so on. However, it always tries to avoid being explicitly warfare-related
- The Lego theme parks are in Billund in Denmark, Windsor in the UK, Günzburg in Germany and Carlsbad, California, USA

Rarities
- Among the most sought-after Lego sets are the *Star Wars* sets, such as the Darth Vader Tie Fighter and the incredibly intricate Imperial Flagship. Collections of Lego *Star Wars* mini-figures have been known to sell as a job lot for in excess of £2,000. A Death Star in its sealed box, complete with 24 mini-figures and Droids, can sell for over £300
- The promotional building sets issued by Weetabix in the 1970s are also much-sought-after, as is the 'Village Square/Main Street' rarity from 1978, which can be found on sale for an incredible £1000+

See also
Official site: www.lego.com
The most weird and wonderful Lego creations: http://www.techeblog.com/
   index.php/tech-gadget/top-10-strangest-lego-creations

Mr Potato Head
The essential: Classic vegetable-based amusement

First appearance of the spud-we-liked: 1949

Current value: Mint-condition and boxed *Toy Story* version from the 1990s can be seen at exorbitant prices, sometimes up to £150. Original figure pre-1990s hard to find, but can sell for under £10 unboxed

Over 50 years old and still going strong today, the potato-shaped character with the detachable organs and facial features has provided entertainment for generations of children. Invented by George Lemer, Mr Potato Head was at first an idea which failed to catch on – the original kits consisted of parts which could be inserted into real potatoes, and toy companies, still in postwar austerity mode, didn't like the idea of a vegetable being used as a frivolous play item. But eventually, Lemer's idea found a home with the Hassenfeld Bros company (later Hasbro). Mr Potato Head was soon joined by his wife, son Spud and daughter Yam. Only in the 1960s was the tenacious tuber replaced by an artificial plastic casing.

His popularity was boosted in the 1995 by the film *Toy Story*, in which he featured as a character, and subsequently in 1998 by his own TV show on the Fox kids channel, which had, as they say, 'mixed reviews'. Rare collectable variants include the *Star Wars* versions such as Darth Tater, Princess Tater and the potato version of droid R2D2!

RetroFax
- Mr Potato Head was the first ever toy to be advertised on TV (in April 1952)
- A million Mr Potato Head kits were sold in the first year
- In 2008, a giant octopus called Louis in Newquay's Blue Reef Aquarium made the news when it formed a strange bond with a Mr Potato Head toy in its tank. Spokesman Matt Slater said, 'We've devised a series of puzzles, games and toys to ensure he's getting the mental stimulation he needs, but Mr Potato Head is definitely his favourite at the moment.'

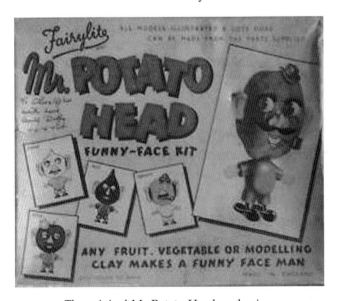

The original Mr Potato Head packaging.

A more recent Potato Head set.

See also

http://www.walyou.com/blog/2010/03/29/mr-potato-head-designs/ for some intriguing unofficial Potato Head designs.

Brooke Bond Tea-Cards

The essential: Mini trading-cards with collectable information

First swapped: 1950s **Ended:** 1999

Current value: variable depending on condition. A set in 'used' condition can sell for between 60p and £2

Buried within packets of tea throughout several decades lay the most extraordinary items; tea-cards, like mini encyclopaedias on various themes. The cards were typically oblong, about 6cm by 4cm, and featured a photograph or piece of artwork on one side with essential information on the other. In the days before Wikipedia and the iPhone, these were portable chunks of information, mini 'applications' to be traded in the playground like illegal currency. Small boys would literally rip open pristine new packets of PG Tips to see if the one card they were missing was inside.

From the 1950s through to the 1990s, Brooke Bond Tea featured various sets of tea-cards on a wide variety of themes, including Adventurers, History of the Motor Car, Wonders of Wildlife and Olympic Greats. The idea was inspired by the popular cigarette cards which had been available before the Second World War. Various topically-themed sets emerged, such as a 1992 Olympics set and one to commemorate the popularity of the cartoon *Teenage Mutant Ninja (Hero) Turtles*. Other available items included wallcharts and albums for which one could send off if one had amassed enough tokens.

The forerunners of today's trading cards and Panini stickers, Brooke Bond tea-cards are sill held in great affection and are collectable if in good condition.

RetroFax
- Cards glued into albums are, as collectables, generally worth less than the sets loose in good condition. It's rare for even a complete album to fetch more than £1
- The first cards, featuring British birds, were produced with the assistance of naturalist and wildlife photographer Frances Pitt (1888–1964)
- An illustrated book, *Brooke Bond: The Classic Tea Card Collections* by Mark Knowler was published in 2009 by Prion Books

A tea-card collector's album.

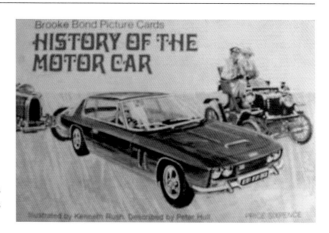

Tea-card collectors took things very seriously, filing their cards in albums.

Timeline

1869   Brooke Bond company started up by Arthur Brooke

1952   John Brooke took over as chairman

1954   Tea-cards began, despite printers initially showing no interest in producing them. The Berkshire Printing Company eventually produced the first batches and Phillips Engineering devised a method of inserting the cards into tea-packets

1968   Distribution of tea-cards had reached 720 million

1975   The popular Wonders of Wildlife series marked 21 years of tea-cards

1986   PG Tips' popular chimp characters from the TV adverts featured on a series of sticker cards

1999   Tea-cards were discontinued when the company took the decision that the interest in them was not adding sufficiently to revenue

See also

http://www.brookebondcollectables.co.uk/ for collectability information.

http://www.teacards.com/gtbrtn/gblist.html for a complete list of sets released in the UK.

Matchbox Cars

The essential: Boy racer dreams in miniature

First whizzed down the track: 1953

Current value: See box below

Sometimes, it wasn't laid on for you and you had to make your own entertainment. Matchbox cars fuelled generations of racing games, competitions and general car-based anarchy, and all without the help of electric motors or any other form of artificial propulsion.

The brand of die-cast toy cars and other vehicles first produced by Lesney in the 1950s has become a catch-all term for the model car in general. Lesney Products was named after its two founders, former export buyer Lesley Smith and business partner Rodney Smith (not a relative, but a friend). When Rodney left for a new life in Australia, Lesley's new partner Jack Odell came in, and, following the postwar lifting of restrictions on zinc, the pair embarked on some imaginative model-making. One especially successful early idea was a gilded model coach sold to tie in with the 1953 Coronation.

The Matchbox cars, which began being produced in 1953, were detailed and accurate models of vehicles with perspex windows, bonnets and doors which opened, and moulded plastic seats inside. Thanks to the success of Matchbox, Lesney Products grew and grew over the next two decades.

RetroFax
- The 1954 Massey Harris Tractor model, issued in orange and red, has rear wheels affixed with screws, leading some collectors to fear they have acquired a patched-up model when in fact this is how the model was originally constructed
- In April 2010, a collection of 2,000 Matchbox cars owned by 65-year-old Horace Dunkley was sold for £100,000. One of the items featured was a 1976 white 1930 Model J Duesenberg car which sold for £4,935 – ironically over £1000 more than the full-sized car, on which it was based, cost to buy new
- The world's most expensive Matchbox toy was sold in Harrogate in 2010 at the Matchbox Clubs 25th convention. It was a rare prototype of the Lesney dumper truck from 1955, and went for over £10,000 to a German collector
- In the year 2009–10, the Matchbox website featured over 100 new collectable cars

Other model lines
- Dinky models included cars, lorries, vans sporting brand names, and even lawnmowers. They were mostly produced on a scale of 1:48, although buses and lorries were scaled down further
- In the mid-1960s, Corgi cars made a big impact with their vehicles tied in to TV and film characters – the James Bond Aston Martin being the most fondly remembered of these
- Mattel's Hot Wheels, from 1968 onwards, introduced the 'low friction axle' – their Volkswagen Beach Bomb, a 1969 model, can fetch over $3,500 in mint condition

How much is that toy car worth?

- A rare green 1930s Dinky Bentalls van was sold for a record £12,650 at Christie's in 1994
- Obviously that's a bit of a one-off, but the rule of thumb is that it's always worth more with the box – it can add hugely to the value. The box alone for an *Avengers* car set, without the cars, was sold for £300
- A 1950s German Shuco wind-up truck, without box, was recently being sold for around £35
- A 1960s Dinky Morris Oxford in mint condition with its box will sell for around £60–£80
- And, at the top end of the scale, a 1948 Dinky Foden flat truck, boxed, with some light marking, was on offer recently for £700
- Other specialist toy car rarities can easily fetch over £1,000
- So there is a huge variety – check out online auction sites for comparisons

See also

Matchbox collector site at http://www.mboxcommunity.com/

www.70er-matchbox.de is a German site featuring galleries of Matchbox cars from every year in the 1970s.

A collectable Matchbox car from the Hero City range.

A 1990s Matchbox car.

http://www.fcarnahan.com/pg/dealers.html#TwoCrazyCollectors   for
    dealer and collector contacts.
www.vectis.co.uk for reliable up-to-date information on toy vehicle prices.

Tonka Trucks

The essential: Durable, powerful and chunky – the essential toy truck

Rumbled into the playroom: 1955

Current value: Mighty Truck prices vary, between a couple of pounds and £20, depending on condition and seller. Expect to pay more for an original Mighty Dump Truck from 1964, restored to excellent condition – as much as £110–£115

There is something powerful, iconic, almost primal about the Tonka Truck. The adult who sees one – let's be honest, we are mainly talking about men here – is instantly transported back to the sandpit and the back yard of his youth, remembering hours of pleasure with those sturdy wheels and that bright yellow tipper.

Tonka started life in the 1940s as a Minneapolis-based company called Mound Metalcraft, making garden implements. By 1955, the Tonka name had been born, and with it the big yellow icon. Their slogan was 'The finest quality at the lowest prices in metal toys.'

RetroFax

- 'Tonka' is a word from the Dakota Sioux language meaning 'big' or 'great'
- Even after the company was bought out by Hasbro in the 1990s, the Tonka brand name remained
- Varieties include the toddler-sized Tonka Wheel Pals, the Tonka Tough for more ambitious play, the guaranteed-for-life Tonka Toughest Mighty, and the nostalgic Tonka Classics range
- In the 1990s, collector Don DeSalle manufactured the DeSalle Collection of Tonka Trucks, designed not to be played with in a robust manner but rather kept lovingly by the serious collector. The 'DeSalle Collection', as it became known, consisted of trucks produced in limited editions (between 100 and 1,500) each with a certificate of authenticity. DeSalle is also the author of *The Collector's Guide To Tonka Trucks* (see below)
- In 1997, Tonka celebrated its 50th anniversary with the 'Tonka Tough Tour', a nationwide tour featuring, we were told, 'a customized 67-foot semi tractor-trailer complete with realistic "trucking" activities, a large play area, an R/C raceway, CD-ROM games, a retrospective of 50 years of Tonka trucks, and much more.'
- In March 2001, Tonka Trucks made it into the USA's National Toy Hall of Fame.

The Tonka Truck ... big, yellow and sturdy.

See also

www.tonkatrucks.net for the official site.

Don DeSalle, The Collector's Guide to Tonka Trucks 1947–1963 (L-W Book Sales, 1996)

Yahtzee

The essential: The Dice say it all

Thrown into play: 1956

Current value: Generally not high. MB Games originals from the 1980s can be found for around £2. The Parker Brothers 'Nostalgia' edition can fetch a whopping (and really rather inexplicable) £35

A dice game promoted by Edwin Lowe in the 1950s and given the big push by the ubiquitous Milton Bradley Games in the 1970s: Yahtzee is basically a dice-rolling game, the object of which is to score the most points through various combinations. The contents – now, steady on, in case this is a bit too exciting – consist of a score pad, pencils, dice and a shaker, all contained within a green segmented plastic box.

The Yahtzee box ... designed to make it look more exciting than it was...

RetroFax

- Legend says that the game was invented by a Canadian couple who played it on their yacht, and so the game was first known as 'The Yacht Game'. The long evenings must just have flown by
- During the ownership of Edwin Lowe, 40 million sets were sold world-wide – and new owners Hasbro claim 50 million are still sold annually today. Who's buying it…?!
- A 'Yahtzee' itself is five of a kind, gaining the highest possible score of 50
- The game is available in a travel version and also a deluxe cloth-bound edition
- Other variants to make it more exciting: 'Triple Yahtzee' (three games at once), 'Painted Yahtzee' (die faces have different colours), 'Battle Yahtzee' (a duel) and 'Pyramid Yahtzee' (tetrahedral dice)
- The Danish dice game Balut has certain similarities to Yahtzee
- Like so much else in the 1990s, Yahtzee became corrupted by the craze of the *Teenage Mutant Ninja Turtles*. A special edition devoted to the ubiquitous green crime-stoppers exists – and it is now so sought-after that it can be found for as little as £1…

See also

www.yahtzee-online.com A dedicated site, believe it or not! Full of information on rules, scoring and strategy…

Scalextric

The essential: Fast, furious electric car racing game, loved by successive generations

Starter pistol fired: 1950s

Current value: New Scalextric Start sets around £60, but sets of classic vintage Scalextric cars sell for hugely inflated prices – £700 or more. Even for a single vintage Scalextric car, boxed and in good condition, collectors will pay £300 and over

The trade mark Scalex first appeared in 1952, to describe clockwork metal racing cars made by Bertram 'Fred' Francis for Minimodels Ltd. But in 1957, a new product called Scalex-electric appeared at the Harrogate Toy Fair – a track with parallel grooves, through which an electric current was carried, allowing cars to move. Initially made of rubber, the tracks began to be made of polyethylene in the 1960s. Now owned by Hornby Hobbies, Scalextric continues to be a popular toy in various forms. A 50th anniversary set was launched in 2007.

Timeline

1957   Scalextric system a big hit at the Harrogate toy fair
1958   Minimodels sold to Lines Bros
1960   First plastic-body cars
1962   New plastic tracks introduced
1964   The now-rare Aston Martin model introduced
1968   Introduction of the distinctive 'pistol-grip' controller
1971   Lines Bros. goes into liquidation
1972   Lines Bros. and Minimodels sold to Dunbee-Combex-Marx (DCM)
1978   Motorcycle models, dropped in the 1960s, now reappear
1980   DCM into liquidation, but management buyout creates Hornby Hobbies Ltd
1999   Hornby production moves to China
2004   Digital racing system, which allows multiple cars on same track
2007   50th anniversary products, including various 'classic editions' based on classic cars, and a limited edition presentation pack

RetroFax

- Bertram Francis ran a tool-making shop during the Second World War, but had always wanted to be an inventor and toymaker
- Francis was diagnosed with cancer in 1985 and died in 1998
- At the peak of Minimodels' popularity in the 1950s, approximately 7,000 Scalex models were being produced each week

Scalextric car. Pure beauty.

Scalextric car ready for an afternoon's static-fired fun.

- Among the special editions produced was one customised around 1990s sewer-dwelling superheroes the Teenage Mutant Ninja (Hero) Turtles on motorised skateboards which can be found in used condition for under £3

See also

http://www.scalextric.com/ for the official site and blog.

www.scalextric-car.co.uk offers cars, spares, parts and track for sale.

http://www.oxonscalextricclub.co.uk/ for a group of 'grown men who never forgot the childhood smells of hot electric motors and controllers, who dreamt of a really long straight and a Scalextric track with more than two lanes.'

http://www.londonscalextricclub.co.uk/ based in Wood Green, London, who say you are 'never too old' for Scalextric.

Risk

The essential: World domination for the would-be table-top dictator

First risked: 1957

Current value: Available cheaply. A vintage 1980s edition can be found for under £3; a 1960s Waddingtons edition for under £10

It may seem incredible that French game La Conquête du Monde was only brought out by the company Miro twelve years after the end of the twentieth century's biggest and bloodiest conflict, but there it is. People obviously weren't averse to a bit of topicality, or maybe this was the Marxist dictum of history repeating itself as farce. Film director Albert Lamorisse, also famous for the Palme d'Or winning short *The Red Balloon* (1956), was the

An early *Risk* box. For dictators everywhere.

inventor of the game, which was eventually adapted by Parker Brothers as Risk: The Continental Game in 1959.

It is essentially a game about winning world territories through warfare. Weapons inspectors and trained negotiators do not feature in Risk – it's armed struggle and war of attrition all the way. The board is a large map of the world, featuring some countries which are now lost in the mists of time. Tokens represent the forces of opposing generals, and the outcome of the game depends as much on the throw of the dice as on strategy. Players attempt to capture territories from one another, and the winner is the one who controls the whole board.

RetroFax
- When Parker Brothers became acquired by Hasbro in 1993, Risk: The World Conquest Game was re-released and slightly modernised, now featuring detailed, sculpted plastic miniatures of Napoleonic-era soldiers. Cards featuring 'secret missions' were added, giving players objectives other than simple world domination
- In 2001, Avalon Hill released Risk 2210 AD, putting the game into a sci-fi setting for the first time. The board is now a futuristic battle-map featuring innovations like a network of underground cities
- In 2002, a *Lord of the Rings* version was released to tie in with the success of the film trilogy
- In 2009, *Variety* reported that a big-screen version of the game was in development. (One supposes that this just wouldn't work for Buckaroo, Downfall or Yahtzee…)

The Hula Hoop
The essential: Perhaps the simplest toy of all

Spun into action: late 1950s

Current value: Expect to pay over £50 for a so-called 'Health Hoop' fitted with magnets. But ordinary plastic hula-hoops are available for just £1–£2

The USA's biggest toy fad ever, the Hula Hoop is also extraordinarily simple – a polyethylene hoop which is twirled around the waist, thighs or neck by body gyrations. It's normally about 28 inches in diameter (children's model) or 40 inches (adults' model). The Hula Hoop is thought to have had its peak in popularity in America in the 1950s, and although its origins are uncertain, some claim the basic principle dates back to Egyptian times, when hoops were made of grasses or vines.

Richard Kneer and Arthur Melin of the Wham-O company (who also brought the world the Frisbee) patented the Hula Hoop in 1958 after seeing children exercising with bamboo rings: 100 million were sold worldwide in that year alone. In 1962 its name became a registered trademark. Interest died off in subsequent decades, but picked up again in the 1990s and 2000s when given a new lease of life by Hulaerobics.

The ubiquitous Hula Hoop.

RetroFax

- A whole new fitness craze called Hulaerobics has arisen out of the Hula Hoop's popularity. It incorporates activities designed to improve muscle tone and posture, and apparently has proven positive psychological effects too...

- The Hula Hoop Marathon Record, for continuous revolution of a hula hoop, is continually being contested and successful attempts are updated at http://www.recordholders.org/en/list/hulahoop.html

See also

http://www.hoopgirl.com/ for the lowdown on Hulaerobics.

The Frisbee

The essential: Flat flying-saucer-shaped disc

Flew into our lives: 1957

Original cost: around 25 cents

Current value: New Frisbees come in many shapes and sizes and cost between £8 and £20. A 'vintage' Frisbee is rare but can sometimes be found for as little as £2–£3

When inventor Walter Frederick Morrison died in February 2010, his death attracted quite a few column inches as he was the man who had brought the world the Frisbee in the 1950s. Newspaper articles were adorned with a wonderfully space-age photo of a grinning Morrison evoking the spirit of Dan Dare in a goldfish bowl-style space-helmet, getting ready to spin his Frisbee off into orbit.

And this is the kind of Zeitgeist the Frisbee was associated with – the whole conjunction of space-race excitement and UFO paranoia. The Frisbee was launched into an America besotted with potential visits from outer space – it's an obsession which has permeated the country's modern mythology, a thread running from the 1950s through to America's post-

Cold-War, pre-9/11 period of inward-looking story-making which resulted in *The X-Files*.

As with many great inventions, the attraction lay in its simplicity. Beautiful, minimalist and aerodynamic, the Frisbee has survived to this day as an outdoor toy, popular with all age-groups, as it is easily portable, quick to get the hang of and requires no auxiliary equipment whatsoever. Just like a football, it can be casually taken to the park or beach to entertain dogs, small children and aged aunts.

Originally known as the Pluto Platter, the toy was sold to Wham-O in 1957. Its change of name was initially informal. Young fans were nicknaming it a 'Frisbie' after the pies made by the Frisbie baking Company of Connecticut – throwing the company's tins around in proto-Frisbee manner had been a pastime of American students in the 1920s. And so, following a copyright-avoiding change of name, the Pluto Platter became the Frisbee. The design was made more aerodynamic by another inventor, Ed Headrick (died 2002) who was responsible for the addition of grooves in the plastic.

RetroFax
- In 1968, the US Navy spent nearly half a million dollars on an experiment involving putting Frisbees in wind tunnels and tracking them with computers and cameras. They also launched them from cliffs to test the prototype of a flare-launcher
- By 1970, Frisbees had become so popular on college campuses that, in some universities, lessons in Frisbee flying were offered
- More than 200 million Frisbees have been sold worldwide
- The Frisbee generates lift as it flies through the air while spinning, thanks to its shape

Better than a cake tin ... the plastic Frisbee, aka Ultimate.

- Scott Stokely holds the record for the men's outdoor flying disc world record distance toss, a distance of 211.32 metres made in Colorado in 1998
- The sport based on the use of a Frisbee, in which competitors score points by trying to reach an 'end zone', is called Ultimate, as the trade-name Frisbee still belongs to the Wham-O company

See also

http://senior-zen.com/blog/news/frisbee-facts/

http://www.absoluteastronomy.com/topics/Disc_golf for the rules of the Frisbee version of golf.

http://www.whatisultimate.com/ for Ultimate rules.

They Said What?
- 'I have as much chance of becoming Prime Minister as of being decapitated by a frisbee or of finding Elvis.' Boris Johnson, London Mayor
- 'He was a nice guy. He helped a lot of people. He was an entrepreneur. He was always looking for something to do.' Walter Morrison's son, Walt, on his father's legacy

---

Barbie Doll

The essential: She's plastic. And, indeed, fantastic

Emerged fully-formed: 1959

Current value: Huge variations according to condition and model. The original 1959 Barbie in mint condition has sold for up to $8,000! Other rarities include Barbie No.4, whose ears were turned green by a chemical reaction, worth between $50 and $400 in mint condition. The 1988 Happy Holiday Barbie has been valued between $400 and $1,000

It's an oft-cited fact that, if the pneumatically-proportioned, eleven-and-a-half-inch tall Barbara Millicent Roberts were a real person, she'd actually pitch forward thanks to the unbelievable ratio between her breasts and hips. She would also be unable to walk comfortably and would have been plagued with back pain throughout her life.

Having recently celebrated her 50th birthday, Barbie continues to entertain generations of girls and, as yet, does not appear to be in need of the aid of Botox, HRT, extensions or veneers. However, most breast implants last 15 years and have been known to sag before that, so, unless Ms Roberts can assure her fans that her ample assets are absolutely natural, she's obviously had a little upgrade here and there. Although, when you are made of plastic to begin with, it probably helps.

American businesswoman Ruth Handler (1916–2002) observed her daughter, Barbara, playing with paper dolls and assigning roles to them. Taking further inspiration from a German doll called Bild Lilli (based on a cartoon character in the *Bild* newspaper), Handler devised the Barbie and made the doll a great success for the Mattel company. Handler became president of Matell in 1967, but in the 1970s was indicted for mail fraud and false reporting to the US Securities and Exchange Commission.

Barbie, though, continued to flourish and became something of a cultural icon. She has changed her look to move with the times, with the Totally Stylin' model even adopting rock-chick-style tattoos.

She has been celebrated in media in many ways, including a painting by Andy Warhol, a New York fashion show, a series of films beginning with *Barbie and the Rockers: Out of this World* in 1987, and a tongue-in-cheek (at least, we hope they were not being serious) international hit single by Danish pop group Aqua. Mattel attempted to sue record label MCA over the latter, but in the Supreme Court of the USA the song was judged to be protected as a parody.

RetroFax
- The original Barbie's measurements, as a human being, would have been 39"-18"-33". These were later adjusted to be slightly more realistic
- Barbie's backing group The Rockers somehow changed their name to The Sensations between the first and second films
- There are over 100,000 Barbie collectors in the world, 90% of whom are female
- A report by scientist Yvonne Shashoua in 2000 suggested that the PVC in early models of Barbie might be poisonous. However, no direct harmful link to humans has ever been proved
- Barbie's first boyfriend, Ken, arrived two years after Barbie herself in 1961. They broke up in 2004, but, in true soap-opera style, were subsequently reunited. Aaah!
- In 1997, Mattel sued car-makers Nissan over a commercial that was seen to use a Barbie-like action figure

See also
http://www.barbiecollector.com/showcase Official collectors' site.
http://barbiestyle.barbie.com/ Celebrating 50 years of Barbie.
http://www.detritus.net/projects/barbie/ The Distorted Barbie – more parodies.
http://www.antibarbie.com/ For the Barbie-hater in your family...

Barbie's Rivals

- **Chatty Cathy:** also manufactured in 1959 by Mattel, Chatty Cathy's unique selling point was, as one might expect, her loquaciousness. A ring-pull activated a phonograph with a choice of 11 set phrases. A vintage Chatty Cathy from the 1960s in good condition (no box) can fetch £60–70. The 'Rosebud' edition from the 1970s is worth far less: maybe £5–£6.
- **Sindy:** Barbie's British rival, created in 1963. Bestselling UK toy in 1968 and 1970, but never cracked the UK market – and redesigned to appeal more to this market in the 1970s, resulting in a lawsuit from the manufacturers of Barbie. Sindy fell out of favour in the 1990s, but was relaunched for pre-school age girls from 2003. Vintage Sindy dolls can be worth £5–£15, depending on condition.

Miss Barbie in her packaging.

Barbie Timeline

1945   Mattel company formed by Ruth and Elliot Handler

1958   First Barbies manufactured in Japan

1959   Debut at the American Toy Fair

1971   'Malibu Barbie' model with eyes looking straight ahead, rather than down and to the side as with previous models. These days she is probably Botoxed

1975   First appearance of the Olympic skier, gymnast and skater models

1980   The first black Barbie, devised by African-American designer Kitty Black Perkins, a Mattel employee

1984   Barbie's 25th anniversary! A 'Barbie and Ken Day' was declared by New York Mayor Ed Koch

1994   35th anniversary celebrated with a limited edition 'Jubilee' doll, of which only 5,000 were produced

1996   The debut of the Barbie website

They Said What?

- 'I think they should have a Barbie with a buzz-cut.' Ellen DeGeneres, American comedian

- 'The doll's image as "perfect" is what most participants disliked most. Both boys and girls said she was too "fake". Barbie has branched out into different careers (e.g., pilot, astronaut) and maintained a sexualized image. The participants explained that the sheer number of careers and her physique make the doll appear phony.' Tara L. Kuther, in 'Early adolescents' experiences with, and views of, Barbie' (*Adolescence*, Spring 2004)

- 'I've done my own calculations and she definitely doesn't have the dimensions of most people, but they are no means grossly abnormal. I'm sure the measurements of baby dolls aren't accurate but no one criticises them.' Writer Moira Redmond

- 'The promotion of dolls with such a body shape, and other things like size zero, have wider public health implications, like an increased risk of eating disorders.' Professor Janet Treasure, expert on body image at King's College, London

- 'If Barbie is so popular, why do you have to buy her friends?' Steven Wright, comedian

---

Gadget Decade: The 1950s

- Transistor radios were first made commercially available
- The Scalextric first appeared
- In 1950, the average house price in the UK was £1,940
- The perfect blonde that was the Barbie doll first made her plastic-fantastic appearance in 1959
- Popular films of the decade were *Cinderella*, *King Solomon's Mines*, *The Lady and the Tramp*, *From Here To Eternity*, *Ben-Hur* and *Giant*
- Rock'n'roll was the new craze. The pop charts began, and memorable long-running Number One singles included *I Believe* by Frankie Laine, *Cara Mia* by David Whitfield, *All Shook Up* by Elvis Presley and *Magic Moments* by Perry Como
- Children's TV began in earnest, with shows like *Andy Pandy*, *Captain Pugwash*, *Sooty* and *Noggin The Nog* still fondly remembered today
- Music show *The Six-Five Special* began in 1957, when the idea of rock'n'roll on TV was still a new one
- Hula Hoops and Frisbees became commonplace

The Game of Life
The essential: Life in a box

Born: 1860 as 'The Checkered Game of Life', but the modern version dates from 1960

Current value: 'Vintage' wooden edition around £35. Standard versions from pre-1980 are not easy to find and can sell for £15+

MB Games had a game with pedigree on their hands when they relaunched The Game of Life in the 1960s, complete with the cartoon version of the beaming face of TV personality Art Linkletter on the box. The Game of Life simulates a player's passage through the various stages of life, from college to retirement – with various pitfalls along the way. (Credit crunches, family skeletons in the closet and middle-class desperation to get a mortgage in the best catchment area are all, sadly, unrepresented here.) Players move along a track through a 3-D landscape, accruing money, prestige and job advancement – with various 'life events' earning them gifts from the other players.

RetroFax
- The 1860 game, created by lithographer Milton Bradley, sold 45,000 units
- Art Linkletter, real name Gordon Kelly, was famous for his TV shows *House Party* and *People Are Funny*

Game of Life box from the 1990s.

- In 1991, The Game of Life acquired a social conscience, with extra rewards being given out for being a right-on do-gooder – e.g. if you were a good little recycler or helped the disadvantaged
- A novelty version is available themed around TV's cartoon family *The Simpsons*
- A CD-ROM version appeared in 1998, which added animation
- The highest sum of money that a player can earn in the current US version of The Game of Life is $3,115,000, which can only be achieved through a very unlikely consistent run of good fortune – landing on all of the spaces which give money and earning the highest possible salary

See also

Rules here: http://www.boardgamecapital.com/life-rules.htm

A mathematical analysis by Wonders of Math at http://www.math.com/students/wonders/life/life.html

Etch-A-Sketch

The essential: Big knobs. Grey screen. Wonky pictures

First sketched: 1960

Current value: Vintage 1960s models are not that rare – some can be picked up for under £5, although in excellent condition in the original box they will fetch more like £25–£30

Design isn't all. An object whose beautiful, sleek minimalism should have seen it survive in the twenty-first century, Etch-A-Sketch is a toy whose time has come and gone, simply because the technology has superseded it. You have to admire the look though – a sturdy red plastic frame, containing a grey screen and mounted with two dials, a black one and a white one. In aesthetic terms, *that's it* – today's toy designers would kill for something so unfussy.

It worked as if by some form of necromancy – indeed, the original French name of the toy, L'Ecran Magique, means 'Magic Screen'. The layer within was composed of fine aluminium flakes, and was scraped back by a stylus when the dial was turned, to form a line. The artistic potential of the thing was pretty limited – it made the Commodore 64's blocky 'Sprite' graphics look nimble. If you didn't want to draw anything which was essentially straight or blocky, then really you were in trouble. And once you had committed your work of art to the screen, there was no way of preserving it. You'd simply give your Etch-A-Sketch a good shake – making polystyrene beads re-coat the screen with the aluminium – and the whole image would vanish forever, like a message on a beach washed clean by the tide.

The Pocket version of Etch-a-Sketch.

RetroFax

- Some reports say an engineer called Arthur Granjean invented the concept in the 1950s, and others attribute the invention to one André Cassagnes. However, the patent rights were held by Paul Chasse, a car mechanic
- The toy was launched at the Nuremberg toy fair in 1959
- In 1986, the Etch-A-Sketch Animator was born as a 'next generation' version of the toy, with a dot matrix display and a limited memory – it could store up to 12 drawings
- A six-colour version, based on the original model, was launched by Ohio Art in 1993
- Artist Jeff Gagliardi became known for recreating world-famous paintings such as the *Mona Lisa* in Etch-A-Sketch form! Jeff's work also included depictions of the Taj Mahal and Chuck Berry, as well as a self-portrait
- Another artist, George Vlosich III, achieved similar fame – his works included a depiction of Barack Obama
- A *Doctor Who* themed Cyberman Etch-A-Sketch was produced by Sababa toys in 2006 – basically no different from the original, but encased in a disappointingly small reproduction of a Cyberman face-plate. A version based on *Star Wars: The Clone Wars* was also produced, as was one themed around boy superhero Ben-10

Mousetrap

The essential: 3-D game and construction amusement

Loaded: 1963

Current value: Vintage 1975 edition complete in the box for approx. £6–£7. A 1980s edition, new, sealed, in mint condition, can be worth £18–£20

Mousetrap, from Ideal (originally Mouse Trap Game) took the simple board game into a new dimension. As counters were moved in the usual linear progression, a construction based on the wacky ideas of inventor Rube Goldberg (or perhaps Heath Robinson, if one is British) took place in the centre of the board – a big plastic mousetrap made up of elements including cranks, gears, buckets and a bathtub. The game has in common with Kerplunk and Buckaroo that it is all, essentially, a build-up to a big, explosive payoff.

RetroFax

- There are 28 building parts for assembling the mousetrap, which have to be taken and assembled in numerical order, if a player lands on a Build space

Mousetrap ... such
fiendish ingenuity.

- Cheese, as one might expect, is an incentive – players accrue Cheese Cards as they go round and land on a Cheese Space
- Each time the trap is set and doesn't catch a player, it needs to be reset. A useful tip is to turn the cranking handle in a clockwise direction, very slowly
- 'The trap is set/ Now drop the net/ Catch a mouse with Mousetrap!' went the original advertising jingle

---

Some of the Rarest Board and Card Games
If you've got these in your attic, go and dust them down – they may be worth a penny or two.
- **Blade Runner:** Made by CPC – based on the film, the object being for Humans to destroy Replicants. Approx £210 for a nearly-mint condition set with some damage, while one in perfect condition can be worth £265
- **Buccaneer:** Sea battle game published by Waddingtons – a mint 1950s edition can fetch £70
- **Drang Nach Osten:** A war game from Game Designers Workshop – worth over £160 boxed
- **Elfenroads:** Fantasy travelling epic, worth approx. £225 boxed
- **Broadsides & Boarding Parties:** An MB Games rarity, which can fetch approx. £180 in mint condition and approx. £90 in good condition
- **War of the Ring: The Game of Middle Earth:** Tolkien-based fantasy game, worth approx. £170 in mint condition

Doctor Who Merchandise

The essential: Time-travelling wanderer in a police box

First materialised: 1963

Main Merchandise: Books, DVDs, action figures, mugs, toys, children's items (bubble bath, lunchbox, etc.) As with any collectables of this kind, being in mint condition and boxed (unopened) will add hugely to the value

That mysterious wanderer in time and space known only as the Doctor first appeared in November 1963, his TARDIS (disguised as a London Police Box) parked in the corner of a junkyard. Two teachers, Ian and Barbara, followed their pupil Susan home (we'd like to see Ofsted and CRB checks giving them the chance to do that nowadays) and found her living inside the impossible TARDIS with her grandfather, the Doctor – upon which they were whisked off into the Vortex for a series of adventures. A couple of hiccups and relaunches aside, the series is still going, with the same basic premise, almost 50 years later. And it has grown from a small black-and-white teatime TV show into a world-conquering multimedia phenomenon. Now, one can't hope to do justice here to the plethora of merchandise released around everyone's favourite time-traveller. There have been books, videos, DVDs, action figures, View-Master slides, lunchboxes, bubble-bath... the list is endless. For the full low-down, see *Howe's Transcendental Toybox: The Unauthorised Guide to "Doctor Who" Collectibles* (2nd edition, Telos, 2003). But here are some of the best items.

Doctor Who Jigsaws (1960s onwards)

Some of the 1960s jigsaws in good condition are sought-after, such as a rare 1965 edition of 'The Dalek's Jigsaw' (the apostrophe is theirs), fetching £175.

Louis Marx Daleks (1960s)

Beautifully produced and pretty accurate, these toy renditions of

Doctor Who TARDIS accompanied by the First Doctor.

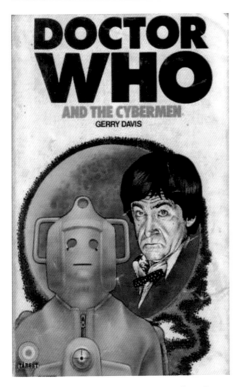

Doctor Who and the Cybermen by Gerry Davis, an early novelisation.

the Doctor's most fearsome foes are among the most sought-after Who items. The black Dalek in its box can fetch £80–£100. The later Palitoy talking Dalek from 1975, which at the touch of a button will offer a series of stock phrases, is worth about £150 boxed.

Doctor Who Annuals (1960s-80s, and again from 2005)

The early annuals produced by World Distributors are a constant source of amusement to fans, as they exhibit a relationship with the source material of the programme which can often be described as, um, tenuous. Characters are brought in which have no relation to the TV show, and there are often pages of filler material about the joys of science and space. The rarest, from the late Patrick Troughton era (1968–69) can sell for £100.

The Weetabix Cards & Games (1970s)

Two sets of *Doctor Who* cards were given away with Weetabix cereals. The drawings and the information on them were pretty accurate, although some of the character choices were a little odd, sometimes featuring minor personages from then-current stories. The second set featured an encoded 'message from the Time Lords' on the back. A complete set will go for between £3 and £10, depending on condition – but the game boards and 'vistas' from the back of the Weetabix packs themselves can command a higher value, sometimes up to £27–£30.

War of the Daleks (1975)

Perhaps the most memorable board-game associated with the show – and one of the oddest, as, dinky salt-pot-sized, pretty accurate Daleks aside, it had little to do with the programme's plots or its main character. Essentially a galactic game of Ludo, War of the Daleks was a rush to the tape – or to the pale blue Dalek Control in the centre of the board. This also doubled as a handle to turn a sort of 'under-board' around, thus moving the Daleks in an attempt to get them to touch your fellow players' counters with their deadly gun-stalks. If they did so, the player was exterminated. The player who made it through to the central control then had a one in four chance of dying again – the central knob contained four cards, all dislodged by lifting Control up. Three of them were large explosions, signifying that you had been successful in your mission, but sadly one of them was a rather frightening King Dalek (not even the fertile mind of Terry Nation had produced that) who could invalidate all your efforts by falling on top of you. Now very rare indeed, and hard to find for under £110.

Target Paperbacks (1970s–1990s)
In the Olden Days, before the advent of DVD and video, the eager *Doctor Who* fan keen to experience *Terror of the Zygons* or *Pyramids of Mars* all over again would have to trot down to the local bookshop with coins clasped in sweaty hand, and part with about 40p–50p for a copy of the 'novelisation' of the TV serial. The vast majority of these were extremely faithful to the teleplay and were written by reliable author Terrance Dicks. The Target novels were hugely popular and sold in their millions, being reprinted right up to the 1990s. These days, nearly everything is out on DVD and/or repeated on BBC3 or Watch – so they are no longer needed. But for a slice of the past – and stories sometimes better told than they were on screen – they can't be beaten. Among the hardest to find are those towards the end of the range which had low print runs, such as the Cyberman story *The Wheel In Space* and Ian Marter's *The Rescue*. Some 1970s first edition hardbacks command high prices, such as a mint condition copy of Jon Pertwee's swansong *Planet of the Spiders*, sold recently for £250.

Remote Controlled Dalek (2005–)
There had been Daleks before, but never like this. Fresh from their appearance in three episodes of the new series, the Daleks, scaled down to 12-inch size, invaded the bedrooms of Britain on a scale not seen since the 'Dalekmania' of the 1960s. The gold remote-controlled Dalek – beautiful, accurate, and with a selection of evil phrases, blue

Doctor Who merchandise went crazy again in the 2000s as the show was revived – note the new series logo on this mug.

lights and extermination noises – was the must-have toy of Christmas 2005. Fans thronged the shops, desperate to find one at all costs, and the lucky recipients spent most of Christmas Day 2005 happily twiddling the remote to make the Dalek parade up and down the living-room, screeching its evil mantras and rotating its dome. Some of them, eventually, even let their kids have a go.

Sonic Screwdriver (2005–)

An old standby – the Doctor's implement of choice, given that he doesn't carry guns. In the old show it used to be able to open locks and scramble the odd control circuit, but in the Eccleston, Tennant and Smith eras it's become more of an all-purpose tool, capable of all manner of weird and wonderful things. Several editions have been produced since 2005, the rarest being the least accurate – that of the Ninth Doctor, with its chunky cream-coloured casing. In its box, this can be found for about £30 now.

The Most Unusual Doctor Who Figures

Over the years, some of the action figures produced to represent the Doctor, his friends and his timey-wimey foes have been, shall we say, less than accurate. Additions to the range which should perhaps have been exterminated include:

- A Cyberman from Palitoy in the 1970s, whose scary blank visage was rather ruined by the addition of a nose
- Leela, the then-current companion in the 1970s, also a figure from Palitoy, who was given some rather amusingly over-styled tresses, suggesting that Farrah Fawcett-Majors had stopped off on Leela's remote jungle planet and had given her a go with her blow-dryer. She also had a good dose of fake tan which would have put a modern girl-band member to shame
- Palitoy also gave us the Fourth Doctor (Tom Baker), who, while he sported a pretty accurate costume with hat and scarf, bore a disturbing resemblance to well-known Avenger and shaker of coffee beans, Gareth Hunt
- K-9, the Doctor's famous robot dog, whose figure produced by Dapol in the 1980s was not the expected metallic silver but rather a somewhat bilious green in colour
- Also from Dapol – the pentagonal TARDIS console. Yes, *pentagonal*. The iconic six-sided prop had, somewhere in the Time Vortex, lost an entire panel of circuitry

---

Radio Times Tenth Doctor Special Edition (2010)
A special 164-page publication produced to mark the end of the David Tennant era, 2005–2010. Won't tell diehard fans anything they don't already know now, but already going up in value and can change hands for £75 in mint condition.

Easy-Bake Oven
The essential: Miniature home cooking

Turned on: 1963

Current value: Recent models, used, very cheap – sometimes £1–£3. Older, collectible versions of the Easy-Bake are hard to find and can cost upwards of £25

Originally made by Kenner Products, his was one of those toys which actually provided an experience above and beyond mere play.

Inventor Ronald Howes (who died in 2010, aged 83), director of research and product development at Kenner, brought the Easy-Bake Oven to the world. Howes is meant to have taken his inspiration from a salesman at Kenner who, upon returning from a trip to New York, asked if Kenner could make a toy version of the city's famous street-corner chestnut roasters. The idea stayed in Howes's mind and he began working on how to create a safe version of this idea, aimed at children. Designed to look like a real, old-fashioned range-style cooker, with a stove top and an oven, it actually worked – cooking dough by means of an incandescent light-bulb. Later, it acquired a heating element instead.

Eleven different forms of the Easy-Bake have appeared since 1963, each reflecting the styles of the day. The most up-to-date version resembles a modern microwave.

RetroFax
- 'We no longer have a garage in our house – it's a physics lab,' Howes's wife said of his tinkering. 'You can hardly walk around in it.'
- Inventor Howes had many inventions ranging from high-tech defence weaponry devices to electrostatic printers. One of his first jobs at Kenner was to find a new formula for Play-Doh, in order to remove some potentially dangerous chemicals
- The 1980s brought a 'dual temperature' model, with which children could cook on 'high' or 'low'
- The Easy-Bake is still being made today, although some front-loading models were recalled in 2007 after it was discovered that children's

The joys of the Easy-Bake Oven.

fingers could become trapped in the oven door. It is now made by Hasbro, http://www.hasbro.com/easybake/

• The Real Meal Oven version, which could bake two pans at once, won *Parenting* magazine's Toy of the Year award in 2003

Operation

The essential: A steady hand required for hospital-inspired fun

First incision: 1965

Current value: Low – easy to find used for under £5

An unfortunate, red-nosed and very worried-looking patient lies upon a table, awaiting the surgeon's knife. He appears to have several nasty gaping holes in his body, inside which an assortment of objects has been – somewhat inexplicably – concealed. The surgeons – or players, for this is a game – have to take their metal tweezers in their hopefully steady hands and remove the plastic objects without touching the sides of the holes, or an alarm sounds and the patient's nose, somewhat surreally, flashes red. The objects, amusingly, relate to the ailment – 'Writer's Cramp', for example, is represented by a small pencil in the wrist cavity, while 'Spare Ribs' are two ribs rather horribly fused together. Players win cash for removal of objects. Game play is controlled by cards marked 'Doctor' and 'Specialist' – the 'Specialist' cards earn the player double money if they are successful.

Yes, it doesn't take long to work out that this is basically a jazzed-up, hospital-themed version of that fiendish 'wire loop' game you get at school fetes. The technology is simple and the appeal, surprisingly, was quite enduring – perhaps because of the combination of being simple to learn, quite challenging to do, open to all age groups and somewhat gruesome. The patient was attached to a somewhat flimsy board, though, and so the game lacked the sturdiness to complement its playability.

RetroFax

- The patient is nicknamed 'Cavity Sam'
- MB Games held a competition for a new piece to be nominated and added to the game in 2004 – the winner was 'Brain Freeze', represented by an ice-cream cone in the head
- Variations included a hand-held version, plus a computer version for the PC in 1998. In the 2000s, a *Doctor Who* version was released in the UK, in which the patient is a Dalek and the buzzer is that dreaded mantra 'Exterminate!' A *Toy Story* version with Buzz Lightyear as the patient also exists, plus a *The Simpsons* version
- The basic principle of the game was designed by industrial design student John Spinello, who created a prototype for an assignment project. His godfather, Sam Cottone, worked for Marvin Glass Associates and brought the idea to the company's attention – initially, the version developed was a miniature 'Death Valley' with the holes being watering-holes. The transformation into Operation came when the idea was acquired by Milton Bradley in the mid-1960s

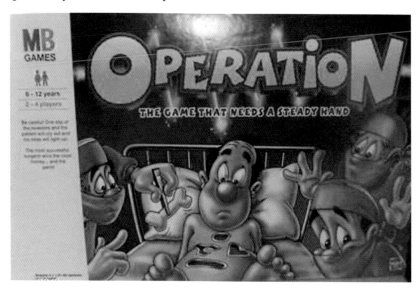

Operation, for the steady of hand and calm of nerve …

Action Man

The essential: Miniature soldier

Swung into action: 1966

Current value: £400 for vintage boxed, down to just a few pounds for newer

Long suspected as a marketing technique for, effectively, selling dolls to boys, Action Man was a permanent fixture in most boys' toy boxes in the seventies and eighties. His grim, set, resolute expression left you in no doubt – here was a man who did not mess around. He went in and got the job done. And he wasn't going to stop for a snog with Barbie on the way, or anything like that.

Action Man was a rebranded import, Palitoy having taken the American GI Joe from 1964 and marketed him for the UK. He went through several changes over the years. His original painted-on hair, for example, became a fuzzy Brillo-pad-like growth in 1970, while 1973 brought the famous

Action Man allowed generations of boys to play with dolls and get away with it.

'gripping hands' which so many of us remember. Later models would bring innovations such as facial hair, presumably so that one could enable one's Action Man to look more rugged after a few days in the desert – or possibly more dastardly. A sideburned version soon took on the nickname of 'George Best Action Man'. The other famous feature, the 'Eagle Eyes', came along in 1976 – these were able to be operated by a small lever on the back of Action Man's head. And the final main innovation came in 1981, with the 'sharp-shooter' position which meant Action Man could now look into the sights of his gun while lying down.

In 1984, Action Man was discontinued and replaced by the smaller 'Action Force' figure, but 1993 brought a revival which lasted until 2006. This relaunched Hasbro Action Man seemed to have lost something of the unique quality of the old figure and to be just another generic toy designed to make children buy as many different versions and accessories as possible – even an evil nemesis, the moustached and robot-armed Dr X.

RetroFax

- In 1996 a special 30th anniversary Collector's Edition in a presentation box came along – the figure resembled the old-style Action Man, only taller and in a deeper shade of green
- And, inevitably, the 40th anniversary figure arrived in 2006. This was made by Modellers' Loft, and was deliberately aimed at model collectors rather than the children's toy market
- Designer Bob Brechin's left hand was used as the model for the 'gripping hands'

See also

www.actionmanhq.co.uk for a comprehensive website with a great guide to collectability.

They Said What?
- 'The problem is they contribute to the idea that guns are normal in our society, and also that they are glamorous and desirable instead of being lethal machines that are designed to kill human beings.' Louise Rimmer, from the International Action Network on Small Arms
- 'The people collecting them used to have Action Men 30 or 40 years ago. They are trying to relive their childhood in a way. They've been collecting them, looking in lofts and in shops, looking for the ones they didn't get when they were a child.' Bob Brechin, chief designer of the original Action Man

Hungry Hippos

The essential: Fun with marble-eating plastic hippos

The hunger began: 1966

Current value: Complete in box for under £5 but will usually be a recent edition. Few vintage versions around now

A tabletop game made by MB Games for Hasbro. The four plastic hippos – Henry, Lizzie (later, inexplicably, Happy), Harry and Homer – face each other across a surprisingly small square red pitch, with their jaws controlled by a human operative. Plastic marbles are placed in the centre, and the hippo heads extend into the field of play to try and grab the balls and consume them. And that really is all there is to it. Apart from the noise. Slamming, crashing, rattling, shaking… this is one of the most volume-intensive games out there. Must make it a great gift for people you don't like very much.

RetroFax
- The original advertising jingle went 'It's a race, it's a chase, hurry up and feed their face!/ Who will win? No one knows! Feed the hungry hip-ip-pos!/Hungry hungry hippos! (open up and there it goes!)' The US version, one should add, features an extra 'hungry' in the name

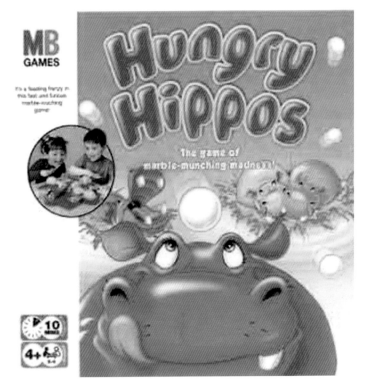

Those Hungry Hippos in a recent box.

- Apart from some cosmetic changes to the board and accessories, the design of Hungry Hippos has hardly changed since its inception in the 1960s
- Play is extremely quick – a single game can be over in half a minute!
- A smaller travel version was produced, with the game arena encased in a plastic dome

Ker-plunk!

The essential: Marble-related fun and tension

First dropped in: 1967

Current value: Vintage 1967 edition can fetch £15–20

Somewhat ahead of its time, the onomatopoeically-named Ker-plunk! took board games into the third dimension. Rather than the movement of counters across a square surface, here was something a bit different; a futuristically-styled plastic cylinder stacked with marbles and rammed with plastic rods ('straws') which were holding them in place, demanding a steady hand and a keen eye to ensure that you would not be the one to cause the great marble cascade. Essentially, it's a game of brinkmanship – how much further can you risk going? How many more plastic sticks can you risk pulling out? The tension grows until, as with Buckaroo!, the final release comes as a pay-off.

The onomatopoeically-named *Kerplunk.*

RetroFax

- Ker-plunk! was made by the Ideal Toy Company and released in 1967. It's now made by the Milton Bradley Company in the UK and by Mattel in the USA.
- Variants include a 'Toy Story Alien Freefall' version with an alien rocket-shaped cylinder – this has an RRP of £15 but can be found for around £10
- The advertising slogan went 'Ker-plunk! is the game where you take your pick and pull a stick. If all the marbles fall, you lose it all! You're only sunk if they go … Ker-plunk!'
- The game included 30 plastic rods and 32 marbles
- An electronic version called Super Ker-plunk Mega Edition came out in 2006

Gadget Decade: The 1960s

- The decade of pop music: long-running Number Ones were *Wonderful Land* by the Shadows and *A Whiter Shade of Pale* by Procul Harum, plus, of course, the many chart-toppers from The Beatles such as *She Loves You* and *Hello, Goodbye*
- The Slinky, first brought to the world in the 1940s, was relaunched in 1962
- The world was shaken by the assassination of President John F. Kennedy in November 1963, and of Martin Luther King Jr. in 1968
- Hot Wheels cars and the Sindy Doll both made their debuts
- Alan Shepard became America's first man in space, and John Glenn orbited the Earth three times. In 1963 Valentina Tereshkova became the first woman in space
- In the literary world, sensations were caused by Jacqueline Susann's *Valley of the Dolls* and D.H. Lawrence's *Lady Chatterley's Lover*
- Top movies of the 1960s included Hitchcock's *Psycho*, the animations *101 Dalmatians* and *The Jungle Book*, and the first James Bond films *Dr No*, *From Russia With Love* and *Thunderball*
- The popular contortion game of Twister first came out
- Making their debut on TV were *Doctor Who*, *The Prisoner*, *Star Trek*, *That Was The Week That Was*, *Top of the Pops* and *Ready Steady Go!*

Chapter 2

Make Me Smile
(Come Up And See Me)

Top Seventies Gadgets

- **Colour TV:** Test transmissions had begun in the late sixties, but the 1970s were the decade of colour – and TV embraced it, with garish hues everywhere from *Top of the Pops* to *Doctor Who*. That didn't mean they were in every home, though – a colour TV set was worth the equivalent of £3,000 in today's money
- **The Teasmade:** At last, the early morning cuppa dispensed at the home-owner's bedside. A vintage Goblin model can sell for over £100 in excellent condition
- **The Breville Sandwich Toaster:** Hot plates clamped together around your bread, buttered on the outside in some strange carnivalesque inversion – it seemed odd. And yet it produced a surprisingly tasty snack
- **The pocket calculator:** As immortalised in the song by Kraftwerk, and brought to the world by Sir Clive Sinclair, who pops up a few times in these pages... His Cambridge Calculator from 1973 finally made the slide rule obsolete. A vintage model can sell for as little as £15, but in excellent condition, and in its white plastic case, for as much as £100

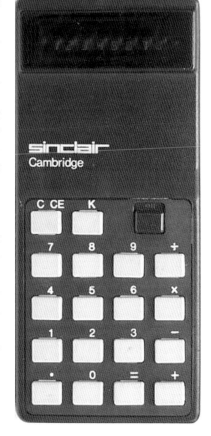

The Sinclair Calculator – vintage models can fetch up to £100.

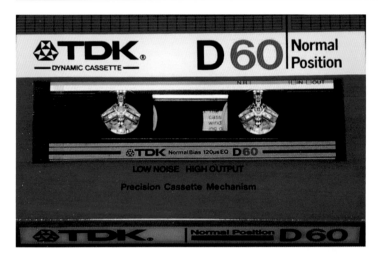

A TDK cassette from the 1980s.

- **Cassette tape:** Mass-produced audio cassettes had existed since the 1960s, but the introduction of Dolby sound reduction and the chromium dioxide tape really made them take off in the 1970s, and in the 1980s the popularity of the personal stereo helped them along further

Spacehopper

The essential: bouncy outdoor fun

Bounced into view: 1968, popularised in 1970s

Current value: Around £150 sometimes, and an original 1970s Mettoy model, boxed, can fetch £200+

With its grinning toothy visage, narrowed eyes and devilish horns doubling as handles, the Spacehopper ought to be a frightening creature, but a tame one is really quite friendly. As long as they are fed and bounced on regularly, they seem perfectly docile. One of those stereotyped seventies toys which are always cited in lazy nostalgia mash-up programmes alongside the Spangles and the Chopper bike, the Spacehopper is nevertheless a genuine icon. Instantly recognisable in its orange rubber livery (although the earliest ones were blue), it has given bouncing pleasure to successive generations of children.

RetroFax
- Marketed in the UK by Mettoy, the Spacehopper allegedly first hit British shores in 1971. However, the Cambridge Evening News was already describing the Spacehopper as a 'trend' in 1969
- Aquilino Cosani (born 1924) of Italian company Ledragomma patented the bouncy device in 1968, calling it the Pon Pon

The unmistakable grin of the Spacehopper.

- Versions manufactured today are usually made in China and can vary in size and appearance. You can usually tell straight away that they are not classic Spacehoppers
- The Spacehopper has also been known as the Hoppity Hop, the Hop Ball, the Kangaroo Ball and the Kangaroo Hopper
- Various world record attempts have been made over the years involving the largest number of people simultaneously hopping in one space. This was up to 1,257 by 2009, established in a university in Mexico

See also
http://www.spacehoppersite.co.uk for a dedicated site

Mastermind
The essential: Code-breaking deduction strategy with coloured pegs

Mind into matter: 1970

Current value: Good value editions can be found fairly easily and cheaply. A 1981 edition can be found for under £1; however a rare Parker Bros version from 1972, for example, attracts offers in excess of £10

Mastermind was one of the 1970s' more brain-taxing board games. It came packaged in a box featuring a dastardly-looking bearded gentleman in a black chair, attended to by a seductive Oriental maiden in a white shift dress – the effect of which was to make the confused buyer say, 'Well, that doesn't look much like Magnus Magnusson, and who's the lady?' There is no connection with the BBC's long-running cerebral quiz-show, although the addictive nature of the game might make you think that, once you've started, you won't be able to finish.

One player creates a 'code' consisting of four coloured pegs in a sequence. This is placed under a cover at the top of the board, and the opponent then has ten attempts to guess the sequence – gaining more clues each time. Each guess is 'marked' with smaller coloured pegs – a white for a correct guess of

The deluxe Mastermind ... the ladies on the box changed but the inscrutable gentleman remained the same.

Word Mastermind – a test of lexical dexterity, only without Carol Vorderman.

colour, and a black for a correct colour in the correct place. It is expected that the guessing player will, Cluedo-style, pull together all the information to form a rock-solid guess before they run out of chances.

RetroFax
- Invented in 1970 by Mordecai Meirowitz, an Israeli postmaster and telecommunications expert
- Mastermind is an endlessly fascinating game for lovers of mathematics and strategy, and has attracted a lot of attention over the years from academic writers. See, for example, the article in *Luck, Logic, and White Lies: The Mathematics of Games* by Jorg Bewersdorff (2004), and Richard Guy's 'The Strong Law of Small Numbers' in *The Lighter Side of Mathematics* (1996)
- There is also a Word Mastermind variant, in which a four-letter word (in the non-obscene sense) is the code to be guessed
- Other variations included a Travel Mastermind edition, the more complex Mastermind 44 for four players, a children's version and the Royale edition (in which two players solve 8 patterns) as well as Supersonic Electronic Mastermind from 1979

See also
An online version at http://www.cyberbee.com/games/mastermind.html

Buckaroo!
The essential: Saddle-balancing and a test of nerve

First saddled up: 1970

Current value: Good and even mint condition boxes from the 1980s not hard to find, priced under £10. More recent editions priced even lower, sometimes just £1–£2

Like Westward Ho! and Wham!, should always be spelt with the exclamation mark present: Buckaroo! is a game of skill and nerve which can actually get quite tense, even though it is so simple it can be played from the age of four upwards. A spring-loaded plastic 'bucking bronco' or mule is loaded up, piece by piece, with all the essentials for a journey into the Wild West and a PC game of Cowboys and Native Americans: a grappling hook, a billycan, a rifle box, a cowboy hat and so on, all lovingly rendered in plastic. You then just have to be sure not to upset the delicate balance of the arrangement – or the spring uncoils and the whole thing jerks upwards, scattering the cowboy essentials into the dust. At which point you utter 'dang!' or some other such clichéd Wild West expletive.

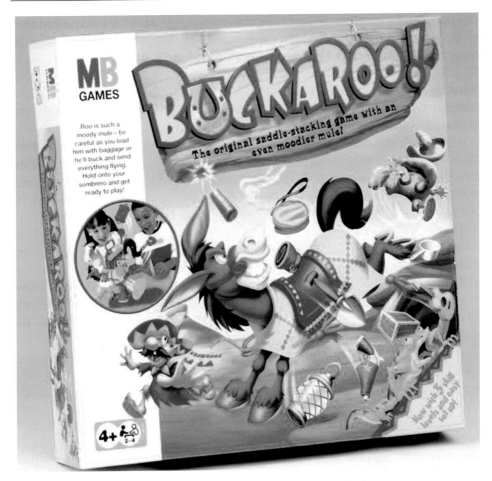

Buckaroo from MB games, in its modern packaging.

RetroFax
- Buckaroo! is manufactured by MB games, now a division of Hasbro
- 'Yahoo! It's Buckaroo! A donkey doesn't do what it doesn't want to do!' went the TV advertising slogan. Well, indeed
- There was an amusing seasonal edition featuring a red-nosed reindeer rather than a mule – called, with crushing inevitability, Buckaroodolph!

Downfall
The essential: Strategy with dials and discs

Rose up: 1970

Current value: £10–£13 for a new Downfall set, used versions of the new game for £3–£6. A vintage 1977 edition can be found in good condition for around £10–£12

The distinctive blue vertical board of Downfall helps it to stand out from the crowd. Looking like a rejected panel from the TARDIS control console, it sports five dials of varying sizes, which contain slots designed to allow small plastic counters to descend if the dials are turned. The idea is to get your counter down to the bottom first – the twist being that you can't see what's happening on your opponent's side of the board... It's a game of strategy, skill and extreme frustration.

It now appears in a new livery, with primary-coloured dials and a more futuristic, arty-looking shape. The overall effect is like something Damien Hirst might produce for the Tate Modern, and is not entirely successful – especially when compared with the stark, beautifully functional minimalism of the original. And it is marketed as New Downfall...

RetroFax
- Downfall was produced by the ubiquitous MB Games
- An oddity of the game-board design is that, while the dials numbered 1, 4 and 5 have the corresponding number of slots, dials 2 and 3 have three and two slots respectively. (There must be a reason for this. Perhaps it is some kind of international conspiracy.)

Inside the Downfall box.

Shaker Maker

The essential: DIY plaster modelling kit

Shook the shops: 1971

Current value: Up to £13–£14 for the more recent themed versions, featuring children's characters such as Dora The Explorer or Ben-10, or characters from the recent entries in the *Star Wars* franchise. Vintage 1970s version rare but not impossible to find, and can often be reasonably priced (under £5).

One of those toys where the effort one is expected to expend seems to exceed any pleasure to be derived from it: Ideal's Shaker Maker was one of those worthy 'make and do' activities. The alchemy involved adding a magic powder to water, pouring it into a terrifyingly orange plastic mould and then shaking it up in something which looked suspiciously like a cocktail-shaker. The end result, after some days of hardening, was your very own home-made statue of (e.g.) an animal, a hippy, a Mickey Mouse, a TV character or a Disney princess. The figure had usually shrunk to about half its original size by the time it was dry enough to touch.

RetroFax
- Shaker Maker was relaunched twice, in the 1990s and the 2000s, by ToyMax and then by SpinMaster

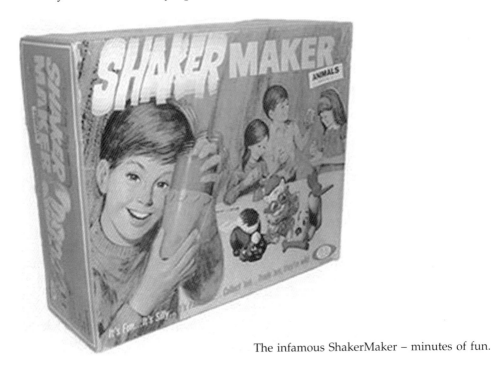

The infamous ShakerMaker – minutes of fun.

- The song *Shakermaker* by Oasis is inspired by the toy, as songwriter Noel Gallagher used to play with one as a child

The Weebles

The essential: They wobbled. And, indeed, did not fall down

Wobbled into being: 1971

Current value: Some examples; Classic Weebles for around £1 each, Playskool Weeble knight and horse £2.50, Fisher Price Weeble Camper Van for under £4

Never was a unique selling point better expressed in a one-line advertising slogan. Everyone, even if they didn't own one, knew what Hasbro's Weebles did – or, rather, didn't do. Thanks to a carefully weighted undercarriage, the Weeble, a small, plastic egg-shaped person, was able to provide literally minutes of fun thanks to its, ah, singular ability. The problem was – what did you do with it then? A number of accessories were provided, all fairly dull. Children, forever versatile and inventive, will have taken Weebles galore for voyages on board the Starship *Enterprise*, battled them against *Star Wars* storm-troopers, engaged them in fights with dinosaurs or simply destroyed them in any number of creative and sadistic ways.

The Weeble's combination of florid pink plastic complexion, shirt-and-tie combo and seventies haircut made it resemble a cross between ivory-tinkling, mother-in-law-hating comedian Les Dawson and darts-player Jockey Wilson. Its narrow, slitted eyes also looked rather sinister – leading one to believe that they were, in fact, small additions to the army of Autons led by the plastic-loving Nestene Consciousness which twice attempted to take over the world in *Doctor Who* during the Jon Pertwee era.

Handsome chaps, the Weebles. They wobbled ... but you know what they didn't do, right?

RetroFax

- Weeble environments available to buy included haunted houses, parks, playgrounds and a Western-themed set-up
- The earliest Weebles were shorter, dumpier and, if such a thing is possible, even uglier, with their facial features able to be constructed out of peel-back stickers
- A Disney set was released featuring Mickey Mouse, the Mouseketeers, Donald Duck, Goofy, Winnie the Pooh, Tigger and Christopher Robin

The Stylophone

The essential: the retro sound of the future

Buzzing away from: 1968–75

Current value: £7–£20 depending on condition

A miniature synthesizer operated with a stylus, the Stylophone was one of the many sources of entertainment popularised by the all-round entertainer Rolf Harris – the man who also brought the Northern Hemisphere the delights of the didgeridoo and the wobble-board, and the joys of giant paintings, making little chuffy sounds with his mouth and making puzzling exhortations to secure marsupials. Rolf's involvement in marketing the mini-synth certainly helped its popularity with the younger audience in the 1970s, and to this day he still uses the instrument in his stage act.

Its origins lie back in the late 1960s when British inventor Brian Jarvis was asked by his niece to repair her broken toy piano. He fitted the piano with

Stylophone packaging. Rolf Harris not shown.

So retro it hurts. The Stylophone.

contacts under the keys to produce an electronic sound, and from there progressed to the idea of the metal pen being touched on to the keyboard to produce the notes.

The eventual device was very basic compared with the electronic keyboards which would follow only a few years later, and the sound was nothing to get terribly excited about. And yet the mere mention of the Stylophone is enough to bring that glaze to the eyes of the thirtysomething, much as when a rent-a-clip celeb waxes lyrical about Chopper bikes and Spangles on some spurious 1970s clips show.

The reason for the Stylophone's popularity seems to have been how easy it was to play the thing. Sliding the stylus up and down the keyboard enabled a fluidity of play which enabled the player to improvise and 'riff' easily. Two basic models were produced – a standard model and the deluxe 350S version.

RetroFax
- Price when new: £8 18s 6d, the equivalent of around £95 today
- The Stylophone was produced and marketed by the British company Dübreq, which Jarvis had formed with brothers Burt and Ted Coleman. The addition of the umlaut and Q in the name were an affectation to make the company sound and look more 'European'

- Rolf Harris was spotted as the potential 'face' of Stylophone after appearing on the cover of the *Radio Times*. TV satirist and interviewer David Frost had also been considered
- Copies and cheap imported fakes, especially from Hong Kong, caused the company headaches
- David Bowie used the instrument on his 1969 record *Space Oddity*, which added to its profile. Other later musicians such as Pulp, the Manic Street Preachers and Little Boots have also used the distinctive buzzy, waily sound of a Stylophone on their recordings.

See also

http://www.dubreq.co.uk/ Company website, with news of the 2007 deal to bring the Stylophone back. For further news of the rebirth see http://gadgets.boingboing.net/2008/01/29/stylophone-reborn.html

http://www.engadget.com/2009/11/23/stylophone-beatbox-electronic-beats-machine-hands-on/ An exploration of a 'next generation' device, the Stylophone Beatbox.

http://www.stylophone.com/Prototype.html For a look at the original 1967 prototype.

The LED Watch

The essential: the future in red digits

First told the time: 1972–77

Current value: A vintage collectable in excellent condition: £270+. A normal Pulsar in good working order and mint condition: £300+. New LED watches in retro style are still being produced and can be purchased for around £45

In the 1970s, the Pulsar LED (Light Emitting Diode) watch, manufactured by the Hamilton Watch Company, claimed to revolutionise the way we told the time. When Roger Moore first wore a Pulsar watch in *Live And Let Die*, it sealed its fate as an icon of cool – but also firmly anchored it to a particular time and place. (This was just before he replaced it with the magnetised Rolex, the one with the magical unzipping qualities.)

The watch strap was chunky and silver or gold, and the face featured a matt black screen on to which, at the touch of a button, the time would be displayed. That's right – you had to *press the button*. The LED used so much battery power that it simply couldn't be kept on all the time. So the key design flaw with the LED was that you couldn't just flick your wrist up and glance at the time – you needed to use both hands. This could be extremely inconvenient if you happened to be, say, climbing a telegraph pole or a mountain face in a rugged manner at the time, or riding a motorbike.

Another problem was the expense. The price of the LED watch put it out of reach of the average consumer – a situation only rectified in 1975 when Texas Instruments began producing LED watches in plastic cases, retailing first at $20 and then at $10 from 1976.

With the advent of its successor, the LCD (Liquid Crystal Display) watch, the LED quickly went out of fashion and soon became a 'retro' item, as much a part of the 1970s as David Cassidy and flares. Modern retro-styled imitations are on the market, some sci-fi styled in a designer's rose-tinted image of the seventies.

RetroFax
- John Bergey, the head of Hamilton's Pulsar division, claimed to be inspired by the futuristic digital clock that Hamilton themselves made for Stanley Kubrick's 1968 science fiction film *2001: A Space Odyssey*
- The Pulsar's claim to fame was not just its futuristic design but also its remarkable accuracy – it was accurate to a few seconds a year thanks to a quartz crystal which oscillated 32,768 times per second. The computer module then translated the oscillations to precise usable increments
- The first ever Pulsar watches were produced as a limited edition in 18-carat gold, costing $1,500
- The designer who brought the first LED watches to the world was Jean Wuischpard, who died in 2006 at the age of 91
- The LED Touchtron, a Japanese model produced by Orient, was a gimmicky variation – the LED would light up if the watch crystal was lightly touched by a fingertip
- Another variation was the Computron driver's watch, which had a slanted screen like a miniature computer terminal
- In the late 1970s, some watches began to combine LCD and LED, such as the Longines model pictured
- Mass-produced calculator watches, such as the Casio Scientific Calculator Watch, began to appear in the mid-1980s

Timeline
1970   First prototypes of the 'Pulsar Time Computer'
1971   Production began with limited 18-carat gold series
1972   Normal production of steel/goldified models
1974   First models for ladies
1975   New brand name 'Omega Time Computer' introduced
1977   Prices reduced because of overproduction in Hong Kong and Japan

Ahead of the game and retro too – the stylish LED-LCD watch.

See also

Some retail sites:

http://www.retroleds.com

http://crazywatches.w.interia.pl/indeks.html

http://www.pulsarleds.com

http://www.theretroworld.com

Resource for watch collectors: http://www.internationalwatchclub.com

A blog on vintage and modern horology can be found at http://www.watchismo.blogspot.com

---

They Said What?
- 'The days of the digital watch are numbered.' Tom Stoppard, playwright
- 'Beeping Casios equipped with mini-calculators and TV remote options, Pulsars with alarm clock functions ... what decade is this? Are we back in the 70s of Clive Sinclair silliness, or the 80s, when every schoolboy and girl, it seemed, demanded size and function over style?' *The Guardian* in 2009, on the digital watch revival

Breville Sandwich Toaster
- **The essential:** Hot sandwich sculpture
- **Toasted success:** 1974 (although earliest sandwich toasters date to before 1920)
- **Current value:** Recent models for around £20, but a retro 1980s model, unused, can sell for £10

The Australian company Breville produced its Snack'n'Sandwich Toaster in 1974, and 400,000 were sold. The UK took a while to get used to the odd idea of buttering your bread on the wrong side and pressing it between two

Staple of a million kitchens – the Breville Sandwich Toaster.

hot clamshell-shaped metal plates. It was a challenge to clean, as well, with fragments of molten cheese finding their way into all the crevices. It also felt disturbingly dangerous, with its theoretical ability to chop your fingertip off and sizzle it to a frazzle.

RetroFax
- In 2005, the *Daily Telegraph* published a list of the 'wasted' gadgets to be found in the everyday home – the sandwich toaster came top of the list, with 45 per cent of adults saying they owned one but did not use it

Magna Doodle
The essential: Etching and sketching, with a bit more freedom

Drawn up: 1974

Current value: From under £1, up to over £20 for a collectable, like a boxed Barbie themed edition

At first glance the Magna Doodle looks like Etch-A-Sketch 2.0. It's a frame full of magnetic particles in a liquid suspension, but where it has the edge

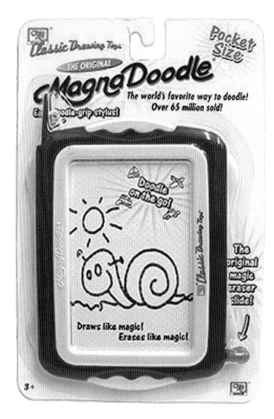

The mini version of Magna Doodle. Not much room for doodling.

over the earlier toy is that it comes equipped with a magnetic stylus-pen (attached with a string, in case you feel like stealing it) so that you can do letter-shapes and more complex doodles. The field of the magnetic pen penetrates the plastic and pulls the particles through the liquid. One is, however, still limited to shades of grey.

Initially produced by Tyco, it was sold to Fisher-Price in 1998. Eventually it was discontinued, and Fisher-Price now produce their own version called the Doodle-Pro.

RetroFax
- The Magna Doodle was invented by engineers from the Pilot Pen company in their quest for a 'dustless chalkboard'
- Although it isn't specifically designed for this use, the Magna Doodle is sometimes used by Scuba instructors for writing underwater notes...
- Various character-themed versions are available, including Fifi and the Flowertots and the usual ubiquitous Disney Princesses. The Barbie edition mentioned above is one of the most collectable

The Rubik Cube
The essential: 3-D maths puzzle

Bamboozling since: 1974 (licensed 1978)

Current value: Difficult to find a genuine pre-1982 Rubik's Cube out there among all the hundreds of imitations, but if you do, expect it to be priced around £60

As the eighties began, earnest-looking schoolchildren could be seen intently studying a toy which consisted of three interlocking layers of cubes, twisting and turning it through its various dimensions with an eagerness bordering on fervour. Rubik's Cube frenzy had taken hold.

Like chess, the Cube was easy to grasp and yet required a great deal of study to master. The puzzle was simple: scramble the cubes up, then try and twist them through vertical and horizontal planes to end up with six sides each of one colour. It was fiendishly addictive, and it seemed like a thing of magic – how could it be twisted and manipulated in such a way without falling apart? A solution to the Cube swiftly became playground currency – and bespectacled young boffins, able to solve the thing with ever-increasing speed, popped up on local news programmes and *Blue Peter*.

It's no surprise that the iconic minimalism of the Rubik Cube is now used to represent everything eighties, on media from CD covers to posters and TV retro programmes. It was actually invented in 1974, though, by

The fiendish Rubik Cube – 1980s icon, although invented in the 1970s.

architecture academic Professor Ernõ Rubik, born in 1944 in Budapest. Rubik's prototype is the stuff of legend, a Heath Robinson-style contraption made out of wooden blocks and elastic bands.

RetroFax
- Rubik himself studied his invention for a month before finding a solution – before that, he hadn't even been sure that there was one
- Initially the puzzle was known as the Magic Cube, but it was renamed Rubik's Cube for the UK market when distributed by Pentangle Puzzles
- There are 519,024,039,293,878,272,000 (519 quintillion) possible arrangements of the Cube
- In 1981, the Cube became an exhibit at the New York Museum of Modern Art
- It was Toy of the Year in 1980 and 1981 (losing out in subsequent years to *Star Wars* and *Masters of the Universe* toys)
- A small market in how-to-solve-it books also sprang up, perhaps the most famous of which was *You Can Do The Cube* by 13-year-old

Patrick Bossert – still available in reprints as late as 2008 (RRP £4.99, but available for as little as 50p from online sources). Patrick turned his skills to management consultancy and now works as a strategy director

- Patrick and his fellow schoolboy prodigies would still have had to go some way to beat the purpose-built robot called the Cubestormer, which solved the Cube in just 12 seconds in 2010
- One of the rarest of the many variations on the puzzle is the Rubik's Cheese. Made in Hungary in the early 1980s, it's approximately 5cm across and resembles, indeed, a small roundel of cheese – or, for those more tuned in to games' metaphor mentality, a giant version of a Trivial Pursuit counter totally filled with all six coloured wedges
- Eliminate the fakes: the best way to spot the genuine article is to look for the Rubik's logo on the central white square – and, obviously, to be alert to alternative spellings used by the imitators, such as Rubix, Rubicks, etc
- In 1982 schoolchildren were allegedly succumbing to a new form of wrist strain known as 'Rubik's Wrist'

See Also

Online solutions now abound, such as 'How To Solve A Rubik's Cube In Under A Minute' at http://www.videojug.com/interview/how-to-solve-a-rubiks-cube-in-under-a-minute#first-layer

And see another, with diagrams, at http://www.scaredcat.demon.co.uk/rubikscube/the_solution.html

Official site http://www.rubiks.com

A modern twist on the puzzle, the Rubik's Slide, being unveiled in February 2010: http://www.technosourcehk.com

http://www.powerstrike.net/puzzles/solutions/rubiks_ufo.htm All about one of the more bizarre variations – the Rubik's UFO, complete with solution.

Instant Insanity
A toy popularised in the 1960s can in some ways be seen as a precursor to the Cube. Instant Insanity, consisting of four separate cubes with different-coloured faces, was a puzzle which got heads scratching back in 1967. The object was to stack the cubes so that each of the sides showed each of the four colours. Invented by Frank Armbruster and published by Parker Brothers, Instant Insanity sold 12 million units.

They Said What?
- 'I do not truly consider myself an icon, but the Cube has been quite successful.' Professor Ernõ Rubik, Cube inventor
- 'The Cube can seem alive as it heats up in your hand. The fact that each face of the Cube is made of three layers of three blocks has an important meaning.' Professor Ernõ Rubik
- 'I cannot tell you what a relief it was to finally solve it. It has driven me mad over the years – it felt like it had taken over my life. I have missed important events to stay in and solve it and I would lie awake at night thinking about it. I have had wrist and back problems from spending hours on it but it was all worth it. When I clicked that last bit into place and each face was a solid colour, I wept.' Hampshire builder Graham Parker, who finally solved the Cube in 2009 after trying for 26 years

Pet Rocks

The essential: Rocks. As pets

Stone me! First adopted: 1975

Current value: Could be bought and sold for about £3 at one time but are not considered of great collectable value any more

The 1970s lo-tech precursor to the Tamagotchi, the Pet Rocks were lumps of stone which needed love. They were the brainchild of copywriter Gary Dahl, whose notion of the 'perfect pet' led him to create the idea of selling rocks, complete with their own gag-filled manuals, as pets. For some reason people got the joke and bought into the idea, and made Mr Dahl very rich.

The Pet Rocks were ordinary stones with cute button eyes, sold (with tongue firmly in cheek) as genuine pets in boxes lined with straw. The manual which accompanied them, running to 30 pages, advised the owner on the care and training of their Rock.

RetroFax
- Gary Dahl's other claim to fame is that, in 2000, he won the Bulwer-Lytton contest for the worst opening line of a novel
- The fad was over by Christmas 1975
- Imitation Pet Rocks flooded the market. If a collector finds one today which claims to be an 'Original Pet Rock', it is very likely to be one of these copies
- The stones used to create Pet Rocks came from Rosarita Beach in Baja, Mexico

- Dahl earned over 15 million dollars during a six-month period in 1975, estimated at over $56 million today. Over 5 million Pet Rocks were sold in this short time
- A USB Pet Rock is now available, which plugs into your computer and... does nothing. The environmentally-friendly website www.treehugger. com voted the new USB Pet Rock one of its top 'eco-toys' in 2010, alongside Eco Barbie in her recycled clothes and a solar/wind-powered doll's house

See also
http://www.petrockpals.com

They Said What?
- 'I remember the exact day when I first got it. I had just unwrapped all of my presents and I thought there was no more to open. Then all of a sudden, mother handed me a small box and when I opened it, there was my first pet rock... I named him Pickles.' Lesley O'Doherty, owner of the world's largest Pet Rock collection
- 'An ideal pet - easy and cheap, and it has a great personality.' Gary Dahl

---

Tin Can Alley
The essential: A little harmless shooting...

First unholstered: 1976

Current value: Available pretty cheaply. Even 1970s boxed sets can be found for under £5

What a strange addition to the toybox Tin Can Alley was. Another hangover from the popularity of the Western, perhaps, in earlier decades? It seemed oddly anachronistic even in 1976, and yet it had a weird, alien compulsion. Cans – bearing the logo of Dr Pepper, another rare thrill – were lined up on a plastic 'wooden fence' and the young sharpshooter would then attempt to blast them off with a rifle-shaped light-gun, an oddly stubby-looking device which looked like the offspring of John Wayne and *Battlestar Galactica*. For a child who longed to be able to fire some sort of projectiles in the garden but was expressly forbidden from doing so by anxious parents, Tin Can Alley was a godsend.

The beam of light impacted on light-sensitive pads, which then triggered small platforms in the 'fence' and would cause the can to fall. The oddity

Sharpshooter's delight – Tin Can Alley.

of it, of course, was that you had to aim not at the can itself but at a point slightly below...

RetroFax
- The face used to launch the game in the USA – and pretty much unknown to kids in Britain – was one Chuck Connors. Actor, sportsman and keen Republican party supporter and fundraiser, Connors had been a star of the Western series *The Rifleman* in the 1950s and so his association kind of made sense
- The game's name was a pun on Tin Pan Alley, the collective of music publishers and songwriters who gathered in New York in the late nineteenth and early twentieth centuries
- Other copycat games followed, such as Marksmen and Electro Shooting Gallery
- The Dr Pepper cans were later replaced with Pepsi cans

Boom-boxes and twin-decks
The essential: Chunky boxes for radio and cassette albums

First switched on: late 1970s

Current value: From as low as under £3 for a used Panasonic from the 1980s, up to £500 for a sought-after mint-condition SANYO M9998K Classic

Popular with breakdancing and hip-hop culture before the Walkman really caught on – so they have a lot to answer for, especially if you know a young teenage relative sporting baggy trousers and speaking in strange grunts. Often seen being carried on the shoulders of angry young men in rap videos, the double-speakered, double-cassette-decked radio is a staple 1980s icon. Today's youths intimidating passengers on the bus by playing them bluetoothed downloads through the tinny speakers of their iPods or mobile phones just don't cut it in comparison. If you really wanted to intimidate the passers-by and make old grannies tut, you had to have a sound-system the size of a small suitcase teetering precariously on your puffa-jacketed shoulder – and the swaggering attitude to go with it.

Of course, they were also the preferred sound system of the perfectly respectable members of society. A radio-cassette boom-box was a quick and easy way both of taping your friend's copy of *Brothers In Arms* (only for your own listening and prior to buying it yourself, of course) and fiddling about with the *Top 40* so that you could have the Pause button ready to lift, vital for getting that New Entry taped right from the beginning without Bruno Brookes wittering all over it. The nostalgia value of taping songs off the

A 1980s boombox ... ready to blast some Rick Astley out.

radio and making your own home-grown *Now That's What I Call Music* compilations is now so strong that there are even Facebook groups dedicated to the pursuit.

The arrangement of the components in a boom-box was simple – loudspeakers and amplifier, radio tuner and cassette decks, all held together in a rigid metal and plastic case and often with a carrying-handle. They could run off the mains, and in theory also from battery power, although they were terribly greedy when it came to the latter, gobbling up Size D battery-power in no time – especially if you did a lot of Hi-Speed Dubbing (copying albums at double speed and slightly less good quality).

RetroFax
- The term 'boom-box' was officially coined in 1981, and refers to large portable radio and tape player with two attached speakers. It's also known as a 'jam-box' and as the slightly less PC 'ghetto-blaster'
- A popular Commodore 64 computer game called 'Ghetto-Blaster' involved a character pirouetting through a street, bombarding the passers-by with musical notes to make them dance
- Boom-boxes can run off a mains power line or batteries – the largest and most powerful models often require 10 or more size D batteries, and running the tape motor would eat the power up...
- New twin-decked models are difficult to locate in the post-CD age. It's just assumed that nobody will want to do tape-to-tape recording any more...
- Cassettes themselves have gone, in just twenty years, from being the dominant music medium to a retro specialist quirk

See Also
BassStation.net, for the future of the Boombox: http://www.bass-station. net/ It's in German, though.
The BoomBox chat area at http://stereo2go.com/6/ubb.x
Some pictures and descriptions in loving detail at http://pocketcalculator show.com/boombox/golden1.html
http://ghettoblastermagazine.com/mixtape/ *Ghettoblaster* magazine still offers free mix-tapes... bless them.
http://www.geekalerts.com/ipod-ghetto-blaster/ Possibly the last word in retro-mania – an iPod docking-station designed to look like a ghetto-blaster. It even has a spring-loaded door like the old cassette units, and separate bass and treble controls! For the serious retro-geek in your family.

Most Important Musical Innovations of the Last 50 Years

1. Sony Walkman
2. MP3 format
3. Apple iPod 1st Generation
4. Compact Disc
5. Napster
6. Dolby
7. DAB Digital Radio
8. Boom-box
9. Sonos Multi-Room Music System
10. Panasonic Technics DJ Deck

Source: *T3 Magazine* (2009)

Star Wars

The essential: Hugely successful, flashy and childhood-defining SF epic

We first felt the Force: 1977

Main merchandise: Collectable action figures, models, bubble-gum cards, the Darth Vader moneybox, duvet covers... It's safe to say it's almost endless

It's easy to see, watching *Star Wars* as an adult, how naturally it lends itself to creative and interactive play, encompassing everything from the 1970s action figures to the modern-day Wii games. The films, especially the original and best, are structured not just like adventures but like games, moving from set-piece to set-piece with strong visual imagery and contained plot-driven narrative. In fact, it's hard to believe *Star Wars* wasn't conceived with a computer-game adaptation in mind (we know George Lucas was a visionary, but he would have had to be extraordinarily forward-thinking for that to be the case).

For the eight-year-old boy who had hardly ever been to the cinema before, *Star Wars* was a revelatory experience, and it's a pity the new films have tried unsuccessfully to evoke the spirit of childhood with their soulless CGI effects and lumpen plotting.

Given that the range of *Star Wars* merchandise is so huge that whole books have been written on the subject, let's just stick to the most obvious examples.

Death Star

Darth Vader's giant battle-station was an obvious candidate for a toy, and even though children might have dreamed of a fully to-scale model, they

Star Wars Lego, a playroom legend in itself.

had to make do with a cutaway wedge built of a gun-turret, a control section surmounted by the retractable bridge over which Luke and Leia do their famous leap (exchanging a not-quite-chaste kiss – worryingly, bearing in mind what we find out later), and the infamous 'Trash Compactor'. There was also a cardboard-and-plastic 'Death Star playset' from Palitoy, which won't have worn well in 30 years... Some are offered for around £100, but it's safe to say collectors have paid vastly more.

Light Sabres
The iconic Star Wars weapon, reimagined as a toy in several formats over the years, from an early version with an illuminated vinyl 'blade' to today's chunky models with compacting 'blade' in green plastic. In 2010, a company even came up with a real-life working model: http://www.techeye.net/science/real-lightsabre-can-set-skin-on-fire

Action Figures
The 1978 Darth Vader with the 'Telescoping Light-Sabre' is thought to be one of the rarest and most collectable, as only a few hundred were ever

The Dark Lord of the Sith ... ready to face Barbie in single combat on the living-room floor.

Luke Skywalker in his macho orange boiler-suit.

made. They can sell for over £3,800. The Rocket Firing Boba Fett is a subject of controversy, with fans debating for years whether the missile-shooting version of the bounty hunter even existed – however, some have surfaced and changed hands for £600–£1,200. At the other end of the scale, less high-profile figures (unboxed) can be picked up for just a pound or two. Yes, Hoth Rebel Soldier, we're looking at you.

See also

www.starwars.com Official site has interesting articles for collectors.

www.starwarstoymuseum.com Site dedicated to *Star Wars* toy collecting, with an incredible three-minute recreation of the film in action-figure form!

Worst Star Wars merchandise

Some truly awful collectables – probably worth hanging on to for the novelty value of their sheer dreadfulness – have disrupted the Force over the years. If Jar Jar Binks made you cringe, prepare to shudder at the thought of:

- **C-3PO Underoos:** the child's matching vest and knickers styled to look like the body of everyone's favourite robot
- **Musclebound Leia:** Princess Leia action figure from the mid-nineties – a bit of a lull in *Star Wars* chronology – beefed up to look like He-Man, and with a scary face bearing absolutely no resemblance to Carrie Fisher's delicate, attractive features
- **Darth Toaster:** The black-and-silver toaster itself, sporting the *Star Wars* logo, is actually quite cool – but it produces a slice of toast with a Darth Vader helmet burnt on to it. How soon would you get bored with the novelty holding it up to your face at breakfast and saying 'I've been waiting for you, Obi-wan. We meet again at last. The circle is now complete' …?
- **R2-D2 Soy Sauce Bottle:** the stubby robot is just asking to be turned into a dispenser for something, and sadly he has been. Look, I'm afraid we've got to say it – May The Sauce Be With You…
- **Yoda Dog Costume:** It now sounds as if making these up, we are. But not making them up, we are. An outfit to dress your pooch as a Jedi Master, there is. (We can't keep Yoda-speak up for long.)
- **Pond Wars Rubber Ducks:** Duck Fader, Princess Layer and Luke Pondwalker, bathtime companions styled to look like your favourite *Star Wars* characters. We should point out in some relief that these latter items were unlicensed…

Other Top Collectable Movie Action Figures

Alien vs. Predator: The so-called 'Celtic Predator' figure, made by McFarlane Toys, eight-inches tall and full of detail like a removable shoulder cannon. Can attract offers in excess of £100.

The Dark Crystal: A prototype action figure – released before the action figures range was scrapped following lower-than-expected box-office takings – recently fetched over £750.

Indiana Jones: the Kenner figures from the original 1980s films are the rarest, 3 to 3.75-inches high – the most sought-after being Indy himself,

Celtic Predator figure.

as played by Harrison Ford, and his lady sidekick Marion Ravenwood, as played by Karen Allen. The Indy figure came with a couple of fiddly attachments – a pistol and a whip. If these are still intact, the figure is a rare find indeed!

A Clockwork Orange: The extremely rare 'Crime Cure Alex' figure, with its accurate costume and sculpting of Malcolm McDowell's face, has attracted bids in excess of £700.

Simon

The essential: Iconic, minimalist electronic memory game

Sounding since: 1978

Current value: Around £20–£30 for a vintage 1970s Simon, boxed and in full working order

Simplicity does not date as fast as complexity. The basic shape of the telephone, the clock face, the vase, the pen... how could one improve on these things? The more fiddly and gimmicky a game, the more it is likely to look dated after 20 or 30 years. And that is why Simon still looks modern. Its simple, elegant design with its bold use of primary colours (a look which some people think may have influenced the logo for search engine Google) suits twenty-first century minimalist tastes very well.

Simon's origins lay in the Atari arcade game which was somewhat creepily named TouchMe. Video-game pioneer Ralph Baer was the man to see the potential in the TouchMe, and brought the Simon to the world in 1977. A handheld Touch-Me (yes, now with added hyphen) came out too, featuring a simpler square design, also with primary-coloured buttons.

'Simon's a computer, Simon has a brain, you either do what Simon says or else go down the drain,' went the original marketing blurb. The simplicity of the idea matched that of the design. Lights would flash up in sequence behind the red, green, blue and yellow panels, accompanied by sounds, and it was the player's job to recall and reproduce them in sequence by pressing on the panels. This was a task which frequently drove the player mad with frustration – and now, a whole new generation of children, plus the young-at-heart, can have a go via the easy-to-find online simulations of Simon which are available.

For its 25th anniversary, the game was re-packaged and re-released as Simon2, a two-sided device featuring the four-button 'classic' side and an

Simon – endless fun, and the inspiration for the Google logo.

The Nelsonic Simon Watch – original packaging. With thanks to Rik Morgan,
www.handheldmuseum.com

updated eight-button side with a choice of complications on the original theme.

In November 2003, 14-year-old Joel Berger of Kansas was crowned 'The World's Best Simon2 Player' setting a Guinness World Record during the Simon 25th Anniversary Championship Playoff at Hasbro Games in East Longmeadow, Massachusetts – hosted, bizarrely, by Donny Osmond. Joel played the longest recorded game of Simon, reproducing 14 consecutive sequences. Joel said, 'This was a cool experience and a lot of fun.'

RetroFax

- The Touch-Me handheld game is now classed as 'very rare'
- Simon featured four large buttons; yellow, red, green and blue. Each button had a different tone. Red (A-Note), Green (A-note octave higher than Red), Blue (D-note) and Yellow (G-note).The game lit these buttons in a sequence and players had to hit the buttons in the same sequence. Game play ended when a player made a mistake
- An official wristwatch version of Simon, with the coloured buttons reduced to small bobbles at the corners of a digital watch's face, was released by Nelsonic. There was even a key-chain version too... just how much smaller could Simon get?
- Simon is associated in popular memory with the film *Close Encounters of the Third Kind*, in which a spaceship, saucer-shaped and not unlike a Simon itself in appearance, emits a sequence of tones to communicate with humanity. The resemblance is, in fact, a total coincidence, but is thought to have helped boost sales of the toy
- In an episode of the animated sitcom *Family Guy*, baby Stewie plays Simon and loses. This scene is noted by fans as being a famous continuity error, as the position of the coloured panels on Simon is seen to change!
- Simon gave rise to many similar toys 'inspired' by it, notably CopyCat from Tiger Electronics, and Space Echo

---

They Said What?
'[Simon] created quite a sensation... It's hard to remember back then how relatively new the personal computer was, or how relatively new even things like a Texas Instruments sophisticated calculator were. We were in our first love affair with the computer chip, and this was the first game that capitalized on that.' Chris Byrne, author of *Toys – Celebrating 100 Years of the Power of Play*

Timeline

1977   Howard Morrison and Ralph Baer file patent application for micro-computer controlled game. SIMON name registered 7 November. Reg. No. 1211692.

1978   The game, now named Simon, is manufactured and distributed by Milton Bradley. Simon was launched at the Studio 54 disco in New York.

1980   Variations of the original game, including Pocket Simon and the eight-button Super Simon, were produced.

See also

Free online versions can be found at http://www.freegames.ws/games/ kidsgames/simon/simon.htm and http://www.neave.com/games/ simon/among others.

The Touch-Me story: http://www.atarimuseum.com/videogames/dedicated/ touchme.html

Touch-Me arcade game is at http://www.arcade-museum.com

Merlin

The essential: Futuristic multi-game

Magically appeared: 1978

Current value: Vintage models are not cheap – can be found for £20–£25

With its distinctive bright red Bakelite livery and chunky phone-shaped design, Merlin looked like a futuristic spaceship communicator, or some kind of device that the Doctor or Mr Spock might have used to reconfigure the contrafibulation wave and save everyone from imminent destruction. It was, in fact, a versatile device containing six games in one hand-held electronic toy – Merlin, the computerised sorceror from Parker Brothers who would encourage you to try and beat him at them all.

Eleven black-and-white buttons, each sporting an LED light, sat on the red casing, above which was a speaker grille and below which one could find four selection buttons marked NEW GAME, SAME GAME, HIT ME and COMP TURN. The games available were:

- Tic Tac Toe (aka Noughts and Crosses)
- Music Machine (making Merlin into a simple sequencer)
- Echo, a memory game similar to Simon
- Blackjack 13, a version of the card game 21 (or Pontoon)
- Magic Square, a pattern game involving switching the lights off in as few button-presses as possible
- Mindbender (aka Secret Number), a game of deduction rather like an electronic version of the board game Mastermind

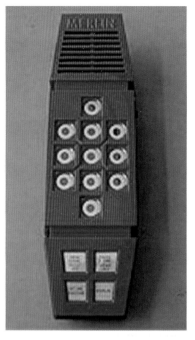

It's fair to say that Merlin was a pretty simple device, underneath its space-age appearance, and it didn't take long to gobble battery-power either.

RetroFax
- 2.2 million units of Merlin were sold in the USA in 1980, garnering it a Toy Manufacturers of America award
- The inevitable redesign and relaunch came in 1995, with a nine-game Merlin rebranded as Merlin: The 10th Quest. A sword-and-sorcery theme led the player through the nine challenges, and if they were successfully completed, the eponymous 10th Quest, involving a dungeon maze, awaited

The many-gamed wizard that was Merlin.

See also
www.theelectronicwizard.com

Speak & Spell
The essential: Patronising home spelling fun

Spelt out: 1978

Current value: A vintage Speak & Spell can fetch up to £25 in good condition, but can be found for as cheaply as £6 if in used condition

Originally part of a set of three from Texas instruments, which includes Speak & Read and Speak & Math (or Maths, for us British). This is the one which people remember, though. A computerised American voice – rather like that of Metal Mickey or the Cylons from *Battlestar Galactica* – would utter the words and you had to type them in on the keyboard for your robotic teacher to mark. Sounds like half an hour of fun. The problem was that, a lot of the time, the combination of the accent and the imperfect synthesising meant that words came out sounding nothing like they were supposed to: when you thought it was saying WORM, for example, it was actually saying GIVE. Yes, that bad. Much more fun can be had with vtech's Alphabet Apple, which can be encouraged, through deft manipulation of its one-syllable keys, to utter rude words.

Literacy in a plastic box –
Speak and Spell.

RetroFax
- The Speak & Spell went through several redesigns over the years, including the raised keyboard being replaced with a voguish 'membrane keyboard' (like that of the ZX-80 computer) in 1980
- Seen as an important popular culture item, the Speak & Spell pops up in various films such as *Toy Story 2*, and is referenced by a plethora of pop musicians. It's also an exhibit in California's Computer History Museum.

Girl's World

The essential: Sinister disembodied head for hairstyling

Heads up: 1978

Current value: Vintage Palitoy models can sell for under £10, but are hard to find now – those on offer tend to be recent versions for £20–25

One of those toys unashamedly marketed at only 50% of children – the clue is in the name – lifesize Girl's World heads popped up on the pink dressing-tables of would-be young stylists everywhere in the 1970s and 1980s. One of their side-effects was to startle younger brothers who remembered seeing the Autons in *Doctor Who*, and for whom a shop-window-dummy head with lifelike stare was remarkably unnerving.

The slightly unsettling Girl's World.

A template for a crash course in hair and make-up, Girl's World wouldn't have passed muster on the average Beauty Therapy course: its plastic hair obstinately refused to stay rolled and its lurid eyeshadow was somewhat unrealistic. Nevertheless, with her artificial hair, painted eyelids, blank expression and smooth plasticky skin, Girl's World may well have unwittingly been the inspiration for many of today's young *Heat*-fodder celebs…

RetroFax
- Girl's World is still made today and comes complete with additional beads (for the Floella Benjamin look), hair-slides and a 'growing hair tress'
- The ever-present Barbie had her own disembodied head for styling, which is also still available in various versions

Guess Who

The essential: Deduction and guesswork featuring amusing cartoon mug-shots and other items

First look: 1979

Current value: £10–12 for a new set, around £17 for an electronic Guess Who Extra. Vintage 1980s versions can be found very cheaply – some are just £1–£3 on eBay

Aimed at children aged six to 12, Guess Who is a game where each player selects a character from a number of mini-mugshots arranged on the board in front of them. You narrow down the choices by asking questions about hair colour, eye colour, apparel etc. until only one is left. It really is as thrilling as it sounds.

As if they'd already realised that the concept lacks a little oomph, the makers Hasbro have, in recent years, added a few ill-advised bells and whistles. These seem about as popular and necessary as the change in the Coca-Cola recipe in the 1980s, frankly. One, called Wild, involves placing pegs beside three of the characters, and gaining extra points if the correct solution turns out to be one of these. Another, called Double, involves the choice of two characters to guess. It all makes *Deal or No Deal* look like a challenging intellectual exercise.

RetroFax

- Variant versions include those involving animals, Marvel Heroes and Disney characters, plus an electronic version Guess Who Extra – and a colour-guessing version called, with crashing predictability, Guess Hue. We're presuming this is, literally, about as interesting as watching paint dry.
- The TV adverts for Guess Who made it look terribly exciting by featuring talking faces on the cards. One wonders how many disappointed children hurled the box across the room on discovering it didn't actually sport this interactive element in real life
- The Danish version won Children's Game of the Year in Denmark in 1989
- Up until 1987, Guess Who had something of a gender imbalance. In the 1990s, feminism took hold of it and ensured equality of opportunity for the Guess Who cards, making the gender split 50–50
- It was also noted in the late 1980s that the whole of Guess Who's cast was white, leading to another bit of rapid rejigging for a bit of 'ethnic diversity'

A 1980s *Guess Who?* Like an ID parade in a box.

- The designers were Theo and Ora Coster of Theora Design, who have been responsible for an enormous number of games over the last four decades

See also
http://theoradesign.com for the Theora home page.

Kensington
The essential: Upmarket strategy game

First on the High Street: 1979

Current value: Vintage versions from 1979 are often not expensive – they can often be found in good condition for under £3, although some sellers can charge up to £15. There was also a computer version (loaded on cassette) for the BBC Micro, which is rare but can be found for under £10

Kensington was much-trumpeted at the time – a genuine effort to create a new strategy-based board game which would, like chess, be quick to learn but could take a lifetime to master. The inventors were Brian Taylor and Peter Forbes and the game was named after the district of London.

The game was marketed in glossy 'upmarket' record-sleeve-like packaging which looked very eighties, and almost space-age with its black-and-red-and-blue colour scheme. The contents consist of 15 red and 15 blue counters and a board with a complex pattern of tiles. The board is constructed of squares and triangles clustered around seven hexagons, three of which are white, two red and two blue. The players first 'scatter' their pieces by placing them in turn round the board, and can then move them along the lines created by the interlocking shapes, with the intention of removing one another's pieces. Forming a triangle of one's own pieces allows you to move one of your opponent's pieces, while forming a square allows you to move two. And that, really, is it.

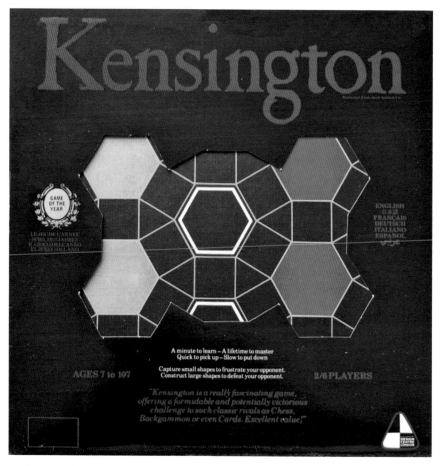

The sophisticated packaging of *Kensington*, designed to blend in with yuppie living-rooms everywhere.

RetroFax
- The general principle of Kensington is quite similar to that of traditional game Nine Men's Morris
- A game called Lotus uses the same board design, but it is more of a 'route' based game in which players attempt to progress their pieces
- One oddity is a promotional edition tied into the wine Blue Nun, featuring the Blue Nun logo on the front of the box. Unopened, this can sell for £8–£10

Electronic Detective

The essential: Cluedo by computer

First detected: 1979

Current value: Around £12–£20 for one from 1979 in working order, boxed and in good condition

The *Electronic Detective*. Miss Marple had nothing on him.

With its futuristic appearance in cream and blue, and its name picked out in space-age font, Electronic Detective really did look, at first, like the next step in crime-solving. For a child who'd already started to have sneaky peeks at *Softly Softly, The Gentle Touch* and *Juliet Bravo* after they were supposed to have gone to bed, this game seemed like the ultimate addictive piece of role-play.

A crime was committed, and a guilty suspect pre-selected by the computer (in something of a Big Brother style). Players would ask questions of the electronic device, and it gave answers on a red LED display (how very late seventies). You would be able to 'interrogate' one of several available 'suspects' whose details were held on index cards, with the aim of getting the accusation right – and if you got it wrong, summary justice was dispensed towards you in something of a *Judge Dredd* way.

This game from Ideal was a brave attempt to enter the 1980s, but seemed slightly sinister, perhaps predating the concerns two decades later about DNA databases.

RetroFax
- The game was designed by Philip Orbanes, game designer and Monopoly expert who is now president of Winning Moves Games
- The suspects had amusing names like Rose Pettle, Pepe Perez, Ling Tong and Al Farook and Lenny Little, all accompanied by simple cartoon mug-shots, minimal biographical details and a selection of questions which they can be asked
- A complete set of suspect cards can be seen at http://www.samstoybox.com/toypics/electronic_detective_cards.pdf

SodaStream
The essential: Home-made fizzy drinks

First popped up: 1979

Current value: One can find them described as 'collectable' with prices up to £10, but more the kind of thing to turn up at your local car boot sale for a knockdown price

An extraordinary, futuristic contraption which materialised in the living-rooms of Britain in the late 1970s, the SodaStream was a device which brought a child's dream to life – making fizzy drinks, live and for real, in the home. Like an ice-cream maker, the machine seemed to involve a sort of alchemy, turning base materials into the heart's desire by adding fizzed-up water to glutinous syrup and producing sparkling nectar. However, children throughout the land were unable to shake a sense of disappointment at the final product, which didn't taste entirely like the fizzy drinks they were used to getting from bottles and cans.

In fact, a system for home-carbonating of water, known as the Apparatus for Aerating Liquids, was first invented by Guy Gilbey (of Gilbey's Gin) as early as 1903, but the SodaStream's place in history as an oft-name-checked seventies retro item is assured.

SodaStream. People actually drank this stuff.

RetroFax
- SodaStream flavours included Cherry Cola, Orange, Apple as Ginger Ale, as well as a variety of interesting combinations such as Papaya-Lime and Orange Mango
- There was even a Vegetable Juice option, perhaps putting it slightly ahead of its time by anticipating the twenty-first century fad for healthy fruit and vegetable 'smoothies'
- The famous slogan? 'Get busy with the fizzy', of course. That's become so retro-iconic that it features on seventies-styled T-shirts
- Comedian Tommy Cooper also featured in the ads, using his famous catchphrase to explain that the SodaStream could work 'Just like that'
- Not to be confused with the Soda Siphon, from the same era, a cross between a Dalek and a fire hydrant which dispensed soda water directly into a glass prepared with a serving of concentrated squash
- A twenty-first century relaunch of the brand is currently in progress…

See also
www.sodastream.co.uk

They Said What?
'People have really strong memories of the brand. There does also seem to be great nostalgia for all things eighties at the moment and people are telling us that they are not quite sure why SodaStreams ever went away.' SodaStream UK marketing director, the optimistically-named Fiona Hope.

Walkie-talkies

The essential: Ultimate long-range communication dream

First switched on: 1970s

Current value: Pricey vintage editions include the distinctive blue Chad Valley *Kojak* set from the 1970s, which can fetch £50+ in its box, and a *ChiPs*-themed version from 1981, also around £50 if boxed. A *Knight Rider* intercom set, boxed, from the mid-1980s, is worth around £25

For some reason, garden and backyard games were given an added frisson if you couldn't see your friends, and had to communicate with them by means of technology. But where the children of the 1950s and 1960s had made do with two plastic cups and a taut piece of string (rumoured to be

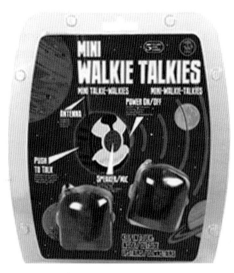

A modern example of a Walkie-Talkie toy.

Cops'n'robbers dreams fulfilled – the next step after the string and two cups.

the basis for the technology which first brought dial-up internet into the wider world in the 1990s), the children weaned on James Bond, *Return of the Saint* and *ChiPs* in the seventies and eighties wanted more. We wanted genuine, crackling, 'over-and-out' walkie-talkie action. And, thankfully, the technology was there for us to have it – at a price. And the affordable ones usually only had a limited range – so limited, in fact, that you might have been better off using semaphore.

RetroFax
- The lowest-cost walkie-talkies were very simple in terms of their electronics, just using a single frequency and a basic transistor
- Some had 'code keys' enabling the transmission of Morse code messages – not usually found on 'real-life' walkie-talkies
- Has remote chatting gone out of fashion? No – the walkie-talkie has just, mostly, been replaced by the ubiquitous mobile phone, with its Bluetoothing and picture-sending capabilities, enabling today's multimedia teen to happy-slap to their heart's content while listening to illegal downloads of N-Dubz. Or something
- Some companies do still manufacture walkie-talkies aimed at children, such as Fisher-Price. Often, these days, there will be an additional film, music or TV tie-in branding – popular brands include *Toy Story*, *Spiderman*, *Transformers*, Bratz and Disney Princesses

See also
http://www.walkietalkiesforkids.com

The LaserDisc

The essential: Next-generation viewing – and a blind alley

Zapped into being: 1978

Replaced: Attempted to replace the VHS and Betamax video-cassette

Current value: Varies hugely according to title and quality, so worth exploring. Some examples of well-known titles: an Indiana Jones three-movie set in very good condition can be found for under £25, Disney's *Snow White* in good condition for under £10, and *Pulp Fiction* 'in widescreen' (but see below) for under £3

Unlike many of the innovations detailed here, the LaserDisc was not a huge long-term hit with the purchasing public. Surprisingly, its first appearance came earlier than one might have expected – the Discovision version was marketed as early as 1978. But it was not until its reinvention as LaserDisc with Pioneer Electronics in the mid-1980s that it looked in danger of catching on.

It seemed like a good idea at the time. Shiny round things looked as if they might be the future. Everyone had known for years that audio cassettes went stretchy and acquired 'drop-outs' after a while, and consumers were starting to realise that VHS tapes were not going to last forever, either. The LaserDisc should have filled a gap in the market.

So, what went wrong? Well, the big, cumbersome 12″ discs, the same size as an old vinyl LP, were perhaps not that aesthetically pleasing. They looked retro rather than futuristic. And some early pressings were subject to a deadly disease called 'laser rot' – essentially an attack by a substandard adhesive glue which attacked the surface of the disc and caused it to oxidise. It was also a noisy format – the size of the things required the machine to work harder to spin them. And some users reported an unfortunate ailment called 'crosstalk', which caused tracks to mix – with hilarious consequences.

So the teething troubles of LaserDisc meant that the world was perhaps not yet quite ready for video on shiny round things. By the end of the 1990s, of course, it would be a different story – the much more efficient DVD system would have begun to replace video cassettes, with a video slot on a home entertainment system becoming something of an anachronism by the mid-2000s.

RetroFax

- The basis for LaserDisc technology had been around since 1958. Dr David Gregg, inventor of the optical disc, originally patented it in 1961

- Pioneer only stopped making LaserDisc players as late as 2009
- LaserDiscs were manufactured for the older TV formats, not modern widescreen sets. So if a LaserDisc alleges that it's widescreen that will mean the picture has been 'letterboxed' – i.e. given that nasty black block at the top and bottom, which film purists seem to love and normal viewers really rather hate
- There were a very few special 'squeezed' disks made with a genuine 6:9 ratio picture, but these were given away with widescreen TVs and were not sold commercially

See also
http://www.lddb.com International database of LaserDisc titles.
http://www.laserdiscshop.com for rare editions.
http://www.dragons-lair-project.com is a source for collectors and aficionados of games on LaserDisc.

The sleek black lines of a Laserdisc player, blissfully ignorant of impending obsolescence.

Swingball

The essential: Tennis on a rope

Swung into the back garden: unknown, but popular in 1970s and 80s

Current value: Vintage versions rare, but can be seen advertised as the 'real Swingball' or 'original Swingball' for around £30

The perfect toy for the Wimbledon summer, as the British waited yet again for their failure on the grass courts to resonate around the world, and for cries of 'You cannot be serious!' to resound amidst the grunts and squeals. Never mind if you couldn't serve like Bjorn Borg or return like McEnroe – the Swingball tennis-ball was attached to a string, in turn attached to a screw-like device at the top of a pole, so you'd have more of a chance of actually getting your plastic racquet within striking distance of the thing. It sounds enormous fun, but could actually be extremely frustrating, as play often slowed to a crawl while the attached line took its time to pirouette back down the screw again, or you had to untangle it from the rhododendrons. Still, there was at least no danger of it going into the garden of the Miserable Bloke Next Door and of you never getting it back.

RetroFax
- An allegedly similar game called Tetherball exists, with a larger ball which one simply hits with the hands
- Swingball is still going strong and is popular on campsites as it will pack away flat into its plastic carrying-case
- Tennis ace Andy Murray apparently first got the bug when, as a child, he used to practise with a Swingball set in the garden. Perhaps the game holds the secret to our future Wimbledon success...?

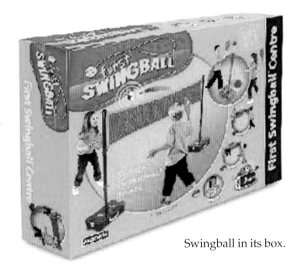

Swingball in its box.

The Ten Best Garden Games

- Gnome bowling: slightly sadistic take on an old game. Seriously, though, does *anyone* do this?
- 3-D Noughts and Crosses: a whole new dimension in wood, adding unnecessary complication to a game which can easily be played with pencil and paper
- Multi-outdoor-games set: for those times when you can't make your mind up
- Giant Chess: a standby of European city squares
- Croquet: an old summer favourite, to be accompanied of course by straw hats, Pimm's and shouts of 'Oh, I say!'
- Turbo Swingball: a twist on an old classic – can still get just as vicious
- Giant inflatable Subbuteo: giant football with its own electric blower.
- Butt-Head: amusing Velcro-helmeted ball antics
- Blockbuster: just a giant Jenga, basically
- Cannonball Drop: scaled-up version of Ker-plunk

(List as nominated by the *Independent* in 2009)

Gadget Decade: The 1970s

- Colour TV arrived, and with it a number of ill-fated fashion choices laid bare on *Top of the Pops*
- ABBA won the Eurovision Song Contest in 1974 with *Waterloo*
- The Stylophone, marketed by Rolf Harris, first appeared
- Pong, the first ever video arcade game, laid the foundations for the video-gaming age that was to come
- Queen's epic album *A Night At The Opera* epitomised the overblown glamour of the middle of the decade, while punk arrived with a raw blast from the Sex Pistols, kept off the no. 1 spot by Rod Stewart
- Swimmer Mark Spitz won a record seven gold medals at the Munich Olympic Games of 1972
- The first appearance of the Sony Walkman came in 1979
- *Star Wars* figures and Legoland Space captured the celestial imaginations of children
- Although the first chunky mobile phones are associated with eighties yuppies, they first appeared in 1973, when Dr Martin Cooper of Motorola made the first ever cell-phone call
- The Conservative leader Margaret Thatcher became the first woman Prime Minister of the UK in 1979

Chapter 3

(Keep Feeling) Fascination

Top Eighties Gadgets

- **The Home Computer:** Whether you had the bestselling Commodore 64, a Sinclair Spectrum or a BBC Micro, the little box which attached to your TV opened up a world of mystery and adventure
- **The Calculator Watch:** They look laughably chunky and unwieldy now, but in 1983 they seemed to embody a future of cool multi-tasking. The fact that Sting sports one on the cover of the Police single *Wrapped Around Your Finger* tells you everything you need to know about the zeitgeist...
- **Mr Frosty:** The novelty ice-crusher with a tendency to jam and break
- **The home video recorder:** VHS finally won the battle over Betamax, and now you never needed to miss an episode of *Robin of Sherwood* or *The A-Team*
- **The Walkman:** Portable music for all, even if you did have to listen to all the tracks in sequence and manually flip the tape over – at least, until Auto-Reverse arrived. (See separate entry.)
- **The boom-box:** Music stereo power with graphic equalisers and a big bass thump. (See separate entry.)
- **The Brother Electric Typewriter:** Briefly popular before the word-processor made it pretty much obsolete
- **Game And Watch:** Hand-held electronic games from Nintendo produced from 1980 to 1991. Each one featured a single game on an LCD screen, plus a clock with alarm. Archive at www.gameandwatch.com
- **The mobile phone:** It was huge and chunky, a laughable Yuppie status-symbol at first. Why on earth would anyone want to tote a house-brick around with them, just so that they could be contactable anywhere? The first time most of us saw one was when it was wielded by Anneka Rice on *Challenge Anneka* – it seemed like something from another world. And now we've all got them
- **Reactolite glasses:** Photochromic glass had been around since the 1960s, but the Reactolite Rapide photochromic glasses hit the USA in 1977

and really took off in the 1980s as a fashion item. Look at any summer wedding photo from the 1980s and half the guests will have their eyes obscured by brown lenses.

The Sony Walkman

The essential: Music for the masses – anytime, anywhere

First spotted: 1979

Replaced: The portable transistor radio

Preceded: Discman, then iPod

Current value: Up to £70/£80 for rare vintage 1980s model, 1950s models around £30

You cannot judge a man by the size of his headphones. Just as men up and down the land compare mobile phones to see whose is the smallest, Sony, the makers of the Walkman, were desperate to come up with some less chunky headphones, as the original model weighed more than the tape unit

A 1980s Walkman.

itself. All very well having people whizzing around listening to the latest hits by the Specials and Blondie attached to their belts, but not if their heads were going to be bowing to the pavement thanks to the ridiculous weight of the ear attachments.

The interesting thing about the Walkman is that the technology wasn't necessarily the breakthrough – portable cassette recorders had been around for a while. Its immediate precursor, also from Sony, was the 'Pressman', a microcassette recorder for the journalism market.

The world was introduced to the Walkman via a dynamic and exciting press launch in the Sony Building in Tokyo in 1979, where journalists were each given a Walkman and given various demonstrations of its sound quality.

The first Walkman was blue and silver in colour and appeared in July 1979. An initial batch of 30,000 was created, which sold out very quickly. It didn't have a record function, which was deliberate. The Walkman was a device for playing music on the move.

These days, nothing changes. We still see people lost in their own little musical worlds, but the headphones are stark and white, like double hearing-aids. The iPod has replaced the Walkman, but it's still used in the same way – just with the equivalent of several shelves of tapes available in its little matchbox-sized box. In just a few years, people have even stopped marvelling at this. In 2009, on the occasion of the Walkman's 30th anniversary, the BBC invited a 13-year-old, Scott Campbell, to swap his iPod for a Walkman for the week. His verdict? He was 'relieved I live in the digital age, with bigger choice, more functions and smaller devices', and

The sleeker 90s Walkman.

couldn't imagine 'having to use such basic equipment every day'. One wonders how antiquated the iPod will appear in 30 years' time, when Scott's descendants are downloading ambient music experiences directly into their heads...

RetroFax
- Sony founder Akio Morita came up with the name 'Walkman', which was supposed to have an international sound and also to tap into the popularity of Superman at the time
- Originally, this was not to have been the device's international name – Sony America adopted 'Soundabout', while the portable cassette player was known as the 'Freestyle' in Scandinavia and the 'Stowaway' in Britain. But 'Walkman' persisted – customers had heard the name and asked for it, and eventually, when foreign sales dipped, the name was changed to 'Walkman' universally
- In 2009, in the week of its 30th birthday, the Walkman was named the top musical invention of the last 50 years by T3 Magazine. T3 said: 'It changed the way we access music, changed how often we could access music, and changed a generation.' The MP3 format and the iPod came second and third respectively
- If you are embarrassed to be seen with your iPod, or worry that it might get stolen, you can now hide it inside a 'retro' eighties Walkman shell. Retropod sells the original Sony Sports Walkman for $100 and the retrofit kit for $20
- The Walkman dodged the controversy about potential damage to hearing loss through listening to music on headphones. At first, little or no attention was paid to the problem, but it was later claimed that listeners were risking their hearing by having the volume turned up to maximum to drown out the sound of the traffic, the gym, or whichever other background noise threatened to obscure the music
- The Walkman sold 50 million units in 10 years and spawned many inferior competitors
- Like 'hoover' and 'biro', the word 'walkman', while originally a specific brand, has now come to represent the general – it is given in the Oxford English Dictionary as a word for any portable, pocket-sized cassette player

See Also
'Just Try It', Sony History at http://www.sony.net/Fun/SH/1-18/h1.html
Many weird and wonderful types of Walkman to be found at http://pocket calculatorshow.com/walkman/sony/ and http://www.walkmancentral. com/for information on Sony products.

They Said What?
- 'The Walkman's gap with the iPod has grown so definitive, it would be extremely difficult for Sony to catch up, even if it were to start from scratch to try to boost market share.' Kazuharu Miura, analyst with Daiwa Institute of Research in Tokyo (2009)
- 'We must make more and more products like the Walkman.' Akio Morita, co-founder of Sony, speaking in 1989
- 'It took me three days to figure out that there was another side to the tape. That was not the only naive mistake that I made; I mistook the metal/normal switch on the Walkman for a genre-specific equaliser, but later I discovered that it was in fact used to switch between two different types of cassette.' Scott Campbell, the 13-year-old Walkman guinea-pig, in 2009

Top Collectable Pop & Rock Action Figures

- **Kiss:** the over-made-up *Crazy Crazy Nights* rockers were released as a set of four PVC figures by the Promotions Factory, each between 3 and 4.5 inches in height. Because it was a Toys R Us exclusive and only available as a box-set, these figures are now pretty rare. They can be tracked down at a not-astronomical £20–£26, though
- **Eminem:** the foul-mouthed US rapper, aka Marshall Mathers, can be purchased in good condition in full chainsaw-wielding action for around £25–£30. One for Stans everywhere

- **Kylie Fever Doll:** A Kylie doll in her silver costume from the *Fever* era (2002) is thought to be one of the rarest items available relating to the pint-sized Aussie pop princess. Boxed and in mint condition, it can demand around £20–£25

Just one of many renditions of musical stars in handy figurine form ... it's the chainsaw-wielding Eminem.

- **Michael Jackson:** Prices of King of Pop memorabilia have become artificially inflated since his death in 2009, and may never settle down again. A 1980s black-and-red statuette featuring his autograph on the base recently went for over £400
- **Madonna:** the most sought-after doll seems to be the one in her *Desperately Seeking Susan* garb, which can attract offers of £40–£50
- **Take That:** A boxed Robbie Williams is, perhaps understandably, the rarest, and can fetch upwards of £50
- **Spice Girls:** Full set of five 'Girl Power' era dolls in nineties garb (including 'Ginger' Geri in her famous Union Flag dress), boxed and in good condition, will set you back £70+. An individual (boxed and unopened) Spice Girls doll is worth about £10–£15

Melanie 'Scary Spice' Brown, cut down to handy pocket size. In the future all pop stars will come to you this way.

CB Radios

The essential: Encoded in-car chattiness

First in touch: 1979

Replaced: The telephone, for a while

Preceded: the Internet newsgroup

Current value: Brand new CB radio starter kits, £60–£90

The philosopher Ivan Illich, in his famous work *Deschooling Society* (1971), foresaw the rise of the democratic exchange of information through freely available networks, twenty-odd years before the Internet found its way into most homes in the civilised world. Illich, describing his idea of using technology to democratise information, envisaged a situation where portable cassette-players would be the future, with people passing these between them almost like a currency of information. 'This network of tape recorders, of course, would be radically different from the present network of TV. It would provide opportunity for free expression. Literate and illiterate alike could record, preserve, disseminate, and repeat their opinions.' He also described a computer-led 'learning web' for the exchange of information.

Illich could have been describing Usenet, or the World Wide Web, or, to an extent, the network of Citizens' Band (CB) radio, which was such a craze in the 1970s and 1980s that, for a while, it looked as if it was going to be absolutely huge. CB is a system for short-range communication between individuals over a selection of 40 channels, and was made legal in the UK in 1981 (although it had, up to that point, thrived illegally). The equipment had already been on sale for a year in the UK, as it was only the use of a transmitter that was illegal.

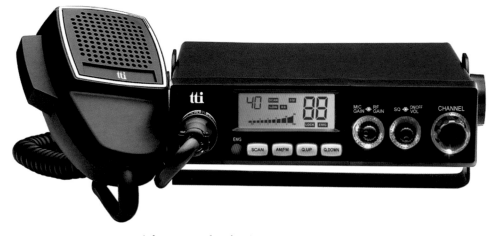

A late example of a Citizens' Band Radio.

The craze started with truckers using their (illegally imported) American equipment and soon spread to a keen network of car drivers as well. Each user would have a 'handle' – not dissimilar to the kind of quirky names people choose to call themselves by nowadays on Internet talkboards and chatrooms. And then they could talk, about – well, anything, really. From the banal to the sublime. The use of slang terms was prevalent, as was the 'ten-code', a system in which the figure ten was followed by a selection of numbers indicating different common activities. The best known, Ten-Four, indicating understanding, can just about still be used today without people looking at you in blank incomprehension. Some other slang terms including 'eyeballing', or meeting up face-to-face, and 'foxhunts', which were gatherings for hide-and-seek activities.

So where did it all go wrong? Well, as we have seen with the Internet, democratising access means you have to take the rough with the smooth. And while the internet community (if one can speak of such a thing any more) appears to have absorbed the small minority of idiots who just want to abuse it, CB users found the idiots and clowns less easy to tolerate. This, together with the rise of new technology, especially mobile phones, meant that CB radio fell out of favour during the 1990s and, by the 2000s, had once more become very much a niche activity. However, the introduction of licence-free CB radio in 2006 saw a reported spike in popularity.

See also

www.citizensbandradio.org.uk

The World of CB Radio by Mark Long, Albert Houston & Jeffrey Keating (2008)

http://www.livecbradio.com/cb-radio-books.htm for a selection of other books on the subject.

Betamax versus VHS

The essential: Feuding brands of home entertainment

Press Play: 1975–77, but peaked in 1980s

Current value: Used Betamax players in good condition from £60 upwards – some as high as £160. Known brand VHS players – Daewoo, Grundig, Bush – for as little as £10–£20 depending on condition

Like Coca-Cola and Pepsi, the two earliest forms of home video are often bracketed together – but where the soft-drink wars are ongoing and the two brands provide healthy competition for one another, the VHS/Betamax war ended somewhat differently, with one clear victor and one on the scrapheap.

Betamax: Sometimes called Beta, this was the earliest form of home video cassette format, developed by Sony in the mid-seventies. At first, it was seen as having several advantages over its rival, being more compact and providing a better picture quality. Another Betamax feature which VHS did not have was APS (Auto Programme Search) or 'bookmarking', where the user could mark points on the tape to avoid the need for constant spooling back and forth.

VHS: The upstart, Video Home System, arrived in 1977. It strolled in enticing customers with a longer playing time and more effective rewinding and fast-forwarding. The eventual winner in the 'format wars' of the seventies/ eighties, VHS won out mainly because of its greater recording time and the value it offered to consumers looking to have room to record two or three films or longer TV programmes on one single tape.

The ill-fated Betamax tape format.

RetroFax
- A VHS cassette can hold up to 430 metres of tape – just over the total length of a standard athletics running track
- A four-hour VHS tape could hold eight hours of material – at slightly lower picture quality and with a few 'tracking' issues – by using its 'Long Play' or 'Slow Play' facility
- In the 'war', manufacturers divided themselves into two camps. On the Betamax side were Sony, Toshiba, Sanyo, NEC, Aiwa, and Pioneer. On the VHS side were JVC, Matsushita (Panasonic), Hitachi, Mitsubishi, Sharp, and Akai
- 1988 was the year when Sony finally threw in the towel and began to manufacture VHS machines
- Betamax production in the USA ended in 1993; the last Betamax machine in the world was produced in Japan in 2002
- However, Kyoshi Nishitani, one of the key developers behind Betamax, still working for Sony after three decades, looks as if he may have the last laugh when Blu-Ray wins out over Toshiba's High-Definition DVD format...
- VHS cassettes are still produced, but the vast majority produced are now blank, as this is the main demand of the market. There is little or no demand for new films or TV shows on VHS videotape any more in the digital age

---

They Said What?
'Instead of poring over the sound and picture quality, reviewers could simply have taken the systems home. Their spouses/children/grand-parents and everybody else would quickly have told them the truth. "We're going out tonight and I want to record a movie. That Betamax tape is useless: it isn't long enough. Get rid of it."...' Jack Schofield, *The Guardian*, 2003

Space Invaders (and other copies)
The essential: Classic hand-held alien-killing

First invaded: 1978

Current value: Space Invaders hand-held game from £5, up to £25–£30 if still sealed in pack. Atari Asteroids game at around £10–£15. A 1980 Invader From Space in box, over £50

To anyone of the right age, the *Space Invaders* arcade game will be recognisable by sound alone. It's that unmistakable combination of the accelerating 'whabb-whabb' pulse and the sharp, piercing whine of the laser-bolts as alien after jittery alien is dispatched with bolts of space-fire. And they grow in number, and they get lower and lower, faster and faster, raining their deadly ammunition on your disintegrating shields until they are so ravaged that they 'cannae take it'... oh, the agony! Yes, it's safe to say that playing *Space Invaders* was an emotional, cathartic experience. But could a

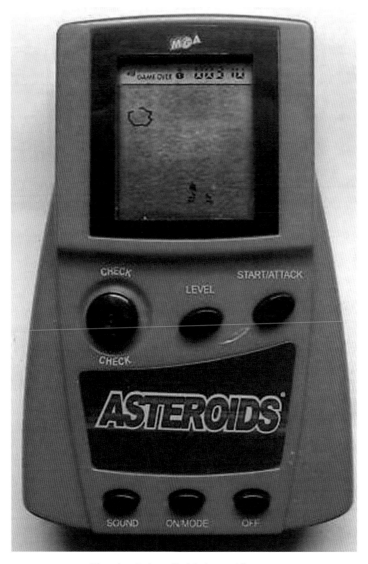

The classic handheld Asteroids game.

Space Invaders in the palm of your hand.

hand-held arcade game live up to that? Well, partly. The minimalist screen and the squinty-small graphics were never going to recreate that total arcade experience. As you stabbed feverishly at the grey buttons, you'd scowl at the logo on the thing and wish that was a tad smaller, and that a bit more space had been given over to the liquid-crystal display. But it was a diverting way to spend an anti-social hour or two.

Other popular hand-held zapping games include:

Galaxy Invader 1000: huge red button and a miniature joystick to wiggle.

Invader From Space: equipped with a circular 'radar screen' layout.

Astro Wars: shaped like a mini-computer and designed to be played on a flat surface.

Pac-Man: pills, thrills and bellyaches in a maze full of ghosts.

PC World's Ten Worst Computer Games Ever (as voted in 2006)

10. *Elf Bowling* **(NStorm, 2005)**
    Supposedly amusing idea, whose appeal is now lots in the mists of time.
9. *Prince of Persia: Warrior Within* **(Ubisoft, 2004)**
    A cacophony of sex, violence and hard rock.
8. *Make My Video* **(Digital Pictures, 1992)**
    A tool for aspiring directors, supposedly, but hampered by off-the-peg clips and dated effects.
7. *Shaq Fu* **(Electronic Arts, 1994)**
    Fiddly, no-fun martial arts game.
6. *Smurf Rescue* **(Coleco, 1982)**
    No fun for kids or Smurf fans, with easy death and an Easter Egg featuring Smurfette nudity
5. *Pac-Man* **(Atari, 1981)**
    How to ruin an old favourite – clunky, shimmery graphics and snail-like pace turn the original slick and addictive arcade game into a head-in-hands experience.
4. *Daikatana* **(Eidos Interactive, 2000)**
    A 24-level, time-travelling shoot-'em-up game which cost a fortune to produce and still manages to be horrible, full of clunking cliché and mediocre challenge.
3. *Custer's Revenge* **(Mystique, 1982)**
    A strange, horrifying mixture of the Western and pornography – and not even a very good one.
2. *Super Columbine Massacre RPG* **(Danny Ledonne, 2005)**
    It doesn't take a genius to see why this is not exactly tasteful, does it?
1. *E.T.: The Extra-Terrestrial* **(Atari, 1982)**
    Slow, clunky and with none of the zest, warmth or spirit of the movie, many gamers rate this as their worst ever gaming experience.

Trivial Pursuit

The essential: Coffee-table after-dinner trivia

First posed the question: 1981

Current value: Over £50 for a boxed *Star Wars* edition. Collectors' editions include the 'Imbibers' Edition' with party glasses, which can be found for around £30–£40 boxed and factory-sealed. A standard pre-1990 edition for £10–£15

Created by Canadians Scott Abbott and Chris Haney, 'Triv', as it became affectionately known, is, perhaps unfairly, one of those eighties icons somehow inescapably associated with the rise of Yuppiedom – an inescapable cliché like having *Brothers in Arms* and Sade on the CD player in your Docklands apartment while munching Ferrero Rocher and drinking Pimm's.

Players move counters around a colour-coded, wheel-shaped, segmented board and, to progress, must correctly answer questions from the 'trivia cards' from a variety of categories: Literature, Entertainment, Sport, Science & Nature, etc. Occasionally, the Sport category would confuse you by throwing in a question about food and drink. Certain spaces entitle the player to collect a coloured wedge, and when the player has all six of these in his playing counter he can progress via the 'spokes' of the wheel to the centre, where the final challenge of correctly answering a random question awaits.

Usually, players agree between them how close to the 'answer on the card' the answer given by the player must be – is 'Thatcher' enough, for example, or will they insist on 'Margaret Thatcher'? Whatever the approach you take, one thing's for certain – it can still, despite the sneer value, be a good evening's entertainment, if you haven't played it so much that everyone's had most of the questions already. Even when you have, there are always supplementary 'Genus' sets of question cards to be acquired. And let's face it – you'll get a lot more intellectual stimulation that you would playing *Deal or No Deal*.

As classically 1980s as Dire Straits on the CD player ... Trivial Pursuit.

RetroFax

- Trivial Pursuit cards are not infallible. *Doctor Who* fans managed to get an incorrect question changed, for example, when it transpired that the game credited the invention of the TV programme to the Daleks' creator Terry Nation
- Another mistake which crept in was the urban myth, put about by a spoof biography, that the bra was invented by Otto Titsling
- In 1984, Fred Worth, creator of *The Trivia Encyclopaedia*, first published in the 1980s, launched a lawsuit against the game's creators, alleging that the questions – typos and all – had been lifted from his book. Worth's ace-up-the-sleeve was the trap he'd laid in his book for the unwary, deliberately misinforming the world that the first name of TV detective Columbo was Philip (when it is in fact not given on screen). Trivial Pursuit reproduced this error. Despite this, the creators were able to argue they had used many sources and the lawsuit was thrown out. The full story is given here: http://www.columbo-site.freeuk.com/firstnamecourt.htm
- There was an American TV version of the show on the Family Channel from 1993 to 1995 – but the BBC's version, hosted by Rory McGrath, came first in 1990
- As with many other board-games, various variants exist. There is a 'Master' edition for the advanced player, a music edition, one for baby Boomers, Disney editions, as well as editions on various decades and aspects of popular culture
- In December 2008, the *Daily Telegraph* reported on the development of a new online facility called Quizbot, developed by technology company True Knowledge, which helped you to 'win at Trivial Pursuit the devious way'
- Chris Haney died aged 59 in June 2010
- More than 90 million games of Trivial Pursuit have been sold in 26 countries, and the game exists in 17 languages

---

They Said What?
- 'God may not play dice but he enjoys a good round of Trivial Pursuit every now and again.' Federico Fellini, film director
- Haney said his biggest mistake was leaving school at 17 – 'I should have done it at 12.'
- 'We didn't know we were successful until we saw a copy of *Time* and found ourselves on the cover. That's when we knew we were in the big league.' Chris Haney

The Sinclair computers: ZX-80, ZX-81 and ZX Spectrum

The essential: Home computers for everyone

Booted up: 1980–82

Price when new: ZX-80 for under £100

Current value: Boxed ZX-80 up to £500 working, ZX-81 up to £200 working

We were promised jetpacks. Or even Jetpacs. A generation of boys weaned on comics and *Doctor Who* and *Star Trek* would not really start to see glimmerings of the world they had always hoped for until the 2000s, when their generation grew up, wore suits, got into electronics and started creating mobile phones which deliberately looked like the Enterprise's communicators and iPhones which looked like their Tricorders. In the meantime, in the midst of sweaty, awkward, pre-teen life, we had to make do with the inventions of the *Guardian* Young Businessman of the Year and Computing's Person of the Decade, Sir Clive Sinclair.

Sinclair is seen as a true British eccentric, an inventor of the old school, never afraid to innovate even if this means occasionally being laughed at. Who can forget the footage of him riding his idiosyncratically wonderful anti-car, the £399 Sinclair C5, through the traffic, hands taut on the controls, knees bent, so close to the road that you fear he is going to come a cropper from a passing juggernaut any second?

But most of all, the name Sinclair will forever be associated with a triad of innovative home computers which brought affordable gaming and programming power to the fingertips of the nation's teenagers – the ZX-80, the ZX-81 and the ZX-Spectrum.

Extraordinarily lightweight – one might even say flimsy – the ZX-80 sold for just under £100 in the UK. Those who felt brave could buy their own ZX-80 assembly kit for under £80. About 20 centimetres square, it had a number of features which made it look and feel totally different to chunky, commercial computers such as the Apple and Apple II. The most obvious was the membrane keyboard, which looked as if it would be touch-sensitive like those *Star Trek* control panels – but which, in practice, required you to put your entire weight on the thing to get it to respond. Incautious use of the Shift key could result in the keyboard slipping across the desk, dislodging the attached RAM pack and sending all of your lovingly-prepared BASIC programs flying into the ether, never to be recovered.

The ZX-80 featured a busy processor which devoted about 80% of its time to updating the video on the TV screen to which it was attached – making it, despite its sleek and minimalist look, something of a lumbering great elephant in terms of computing speed. Its multifunctional keys meant that whole BASIC commands could be entered at one touch, and its infamous 'Syntax check' would ensure there were no errors in the programming.

The home computing revolution began here. The ZX-80.

Its 1K of RAM was something of a disadvantage – only very short programs would fit into that kind of memory. Thankfully, memory add-ons were available in the form of the aforementioned RAM packs. These could literally be plugged into the back of the computer and at first were available in sizes ranging from an extra 1K to 3K. However, as the prices of chips became more realistic, Sinclair began offering 16K RAM packs.

The ZX-81, which came along a year later, had a more efficient processor with 'flicker free' mode, and a look which Spinal Tap might have described as 'none more black'. It looked a bit more sci-fi and 1980s, and a little less like a piece of left-over Bakelite with some typewriter keys attached to it. The membrane keyboard was still in place, meaning that enthusiastic tappers had to keep an eye on the screen at all times to make sure that the key had responded – there was no reassuring click.

Young designer Rick Dickinson was the man responsible for the sleek look of the ZX-81, which he produced in about six months. In-house industrial designer at Sinclair, whizz-kid Dickinson was a graduate of Newcastle Polytechnic who joined Sinclair before he had even finished his degree. He was also something of a perfectionist. Speaking in 1982, Dickinson said, 'I don't think I have ever been delighted with anything I have done. There always seems to be room for improvement.'

Upgrade! The ZX-81, next stage in home computing.

The eager young computer buff could find BASIC coding for games in such magazines as *Sinclair User*, but they were inevitably rather disappointing – a game with a terrifically exciting name like 'Lunar Lander' proved, on loading, to consist of a $ sign moving horizontally across the screen, controlled by the Z and X keys (do you see what they did there?).

The ZX Spectrum was a step up again. Speaking in *Sinclair User* in 1982, Dickinson said, 'I like the Spectrum much more than the ZX-81. It was much quicker to design but much more complicated. It is a step upmarket and I was really trying hard for a super-smart machine. It is not for quite the same amateur market.'

If the ZX-81 looked like something years ahead of its older brother, then the Spectrum seemed to have emerged from another decade. About the size of a large paperback book, it was sleek and black with a distinctive rainbow flash in the bottom right-hand corner. And the keys were raised – albeit made of rubber, so still with a somewhat flimsy feel that set the machine apart from chunkier-keyboarded home computers like the Commodore VIC-20 and the Dragon 32. The Spectrum's two big draws were its colour display and its greater memory power – even the bog-standard model (of the eight available) featured 16Kb of RAM, enough to write a decent BASIC program and run some pretty impressive-looking games. Young computing fans everywhere didn't take much persuading to upgrade.

The standard piece of storage equipment which one could link up to the Spectrum was the audio cassette tape. And pretty soon, software companies were falling over themselves to write games and other entertaining programs

For many, Sinclair's masterpiece – the Spectrum.

for the machine – all available in handy cassette packs. One only has to mention the names *Jetpac*, *Manic Miner* or *Hobbit* to any thirtysomething computer buff and to see their eyes glaze over with joy. Other popular games included:

Galaxians: They were *Space Invaders* who could swoop!
Hungry Horace: Cartoon figure who played cat-and-mouse games in a maze.
Arcadia: Epic space battles from Imagine software.

The elephant in the room, though, is the pirated tape. In the days before file-sharing, schoolboys up and down the land had mastered the art of High Speed Dubbing – nothing to do with cleaning their football boots, but rather the setting on their twin-deck cassette-players which enabled expensive cassette games to be copied to blank cassettes for mates. The price – one game in return. The software companies might have known this went on, but there was nothing they could do about it.

RetroFax

- The sloth of the ZX-80 was legendary. When running a BASIC program, the display would black out while the processor was busy. This made moving graphics difficult as the program would be constantly intro-ducing pauses to keep up with the requirements
- Another problem with the ZX-80 was its tendency to overheat
- Spectrum fans like to refer to themselves as 'Specchums'

- The life of the ZX Spectrum officially ended in 1988, although various computing groups and magazines kept its alive for a couple more years. It then passed into the collective memory, and is now a huge part of the computer nostalgia vogue on the internet
- 'The power of the Sinclair ZX Spectrum comes from a new 16K BASIC ROM. So, in addition to the features of the ZX-81, the ZX Spectrum gives you a full 8 colours, a sound generator, high-resolution graphics and many other features – including the facility to support separate datafiles.' From Sinclair's original promotional brochure
- Amstrad eventually bought Sinclair out, and its attempts in the late 1980s to produce updated versions of the Spectrum met with a lukewarm response – largely because, in a market where the Amiga games console was taking over, the new Spectrums were seen as poor value for money
- After the budget ZX-80 and ZX-81 paved the way, some of the most popular home computers were the Commodore Vic-20 and Commodore 64, the Dragon 32 and the ZX Spectrum. The BBC Micro was the choice for schools. The Commodore 64 was the biggest seller overall, with 17 million sold between August 1982 and April 1994

See also
http://home.micros.users.btopenworld.com/zx80/zx80.html How to build your own ZX-80 and ZX-81!
http://web.ukonline.co.uk/sinclair.zx81/ A downloadable programming manual.
http://www.worldofspectrum.org/ Featuring, among many other things, an archive of games.
More games at http://www.zxspectrum.net/

For a photo gallery see
http://www.nvg.ntnu.no/sinclair/computers/zxspectrum/spec_photos.htm
Sinclair User magazine archive at http://www.sincuser.f9.co.uk/
See also the archive of *Crash*, the ZX Spectrum magazine at http://www.crashonline.org.uk/

Sinclair User (1982–93) **Publisher: EMAP**
The magazine was aimed at the serious hobbyist and covered much more than just home gaming. It also dealt with business and education applications. In 1986, it was repositioned as a games magazine to contend with its main rival, *Your Sinclair*. The extra cost of free tape giveaways began to eat into the magazine's overheads. Eventually its falling circulation brought about its demise in 1993.

The Care Bears

The essential: Oddly unattractive multi-coloured bears with a range of accessories and merchandise

Hugged into life: 1982

Current value: 1980s soft toys for as little as £5, up to £15 in good condition. Plastic poseable figures for around £7–£10 depending on condition

Created in 1981 for a range of greetings cards, the lurid Care Bears soon hugged their way into public affection despite not really looking all that loveable. They were brought to life by designer Muriel Fahrion, who had also brought the world the cloying character Strawberry Shortcake. A range of soft toys produced by Parker Brothers, the Bears went on to star in their own TV and film series. Care Bears merchandise includes books, T-shirts, mugs, photo frames, sticker books, scribble pads, shoes and more.

RetroFax

- The Care Bears craze died away at the end of the 1980s – however, the nineties saw an attempt to relaunch them with an environmentally-friendly twist
- For their 20th anniversary in 2002, the Care bears were relaunched again, this time with a new look

The really rather unsettling Care Bears.

- The Bears' ultimate weapon is the Care Bear Stare. It's more than a rival for the Hard Stare as perfected by Paddington Bear – it's a kind of communal hypnosis in which the Bears stand together and emit beams of light from their magical tummy-symbols, bringing joy into the heart of the victim
- One of the rarest pieces of Care Bears merchandise is the video game made for the Atari 2600 in 1983. With very simple, chunky graphics, it would have revolved around grabbing the 'tummy icon' from each of the Bears as they descended from the screen. The game was cancelled after beta-testing and never made commercially available, on the grounds that the market was shrinking and the play was too uninteresting. It only exists as a prototype
- Care Bears merchandise also ventured into the educational realm, with various interactive toys like the Care-a-Lot Learning Centre

Fighting Fantasy Gamebooks

The essential: A novel in which you are the hero and you choose the direction of the plot – postmodern interactive *Dungeons & Dragons* for the pre-Internet age

The dungeon opened: 1982

Price when new: *The Warlock of Firetop Mountain* priced at £1.50

Current value: Early editions do not appear to be that rare, and can be found on collectors' sites for between £1 and £4 each depending on condition. A sought-after edition is the 25th anniversary edition of *Warlock*, which changes hands for around £8

The names Steve Jackson and Ian Livingstone reverberate through the lives of a large number of boys who were teenagers in the 1980s, weaned on *Lord of the Rings* and not quite ready to discover girls – well, not unless they were fearless warrior-girls clad in mail, armed with a magical staff and sporting a SKILL score of 11 and a STAMINA of 23.

For Mr Jackson and Mr Livingstone did the seemingly impossible, and condensed the recondite, intricate world of the *Dungeons and Dragons*-type fantasy role playing game into an easily-digestible, portable paperback book – one the length of the average novel for older children. Fighting Fantasy books effortlessly created a world in a few brief descriptive passages, and then launched the hero – you, the reader – into a breathless adventure in which your trusty weapons were a pencil, a piece of paper and two dice. It really was that simple.

Dungeons and Dragons

Role-playing game devised by Gary Gygax and Dave Arneson in 1974, and a staple of school lunchtime and after-school clubs throughout the world. Players roll dice to create characters with a balance of Strength, Constitution, Dexterity, Intelligence, Wisdom, and Charisma. The Games-master, who has all of the information on the dungeon environment in front of him, controls the action, and determines the outcome of risky actions by rolling dice. Along the way, players encounter mysterious objects, helpful assistants and ravenous beasts.

The Fighting Fantasy series had humble beginnings. Jackson and Livingstone, founders of the Games Workshop company, got together with Penguin Books editor Geraldine Cooke and came up, initially, with the idea of a Fantasy Role-playing Manual. This quickly evolved into a more exciting idea – a game within a book, in which the moves were simulated by the rolling of the dice and the turning of the pages.

Jackson and Livingstone split the writing of the book down the middle between them, and after a rewrite to ensure stylistic consistency, delivered the manuscript to Penguin, where it was published as a Puffin book. Initially called *The Magic Quest* before acquiring its final title of *The Warlock of Firetop Mountain*, the first book in the series was to become a gradual word-of-mouth hit – and, despite having its brickbats from groups such as the Evangelical Alliance, it also gained acclaim for helping 'reluctant readers'.

The books rapidly developed into a series. Further fantasy environments were created to explore in the form of *The Citadel of Chaos* and *The Forest of Doom*, and these were followed rapidly by others such as *Deathtrap Dungeon* and *Island of the Lizard King*. Jackson and Livingstone didn't mess about with the winning formula – except perhaps on the less successful *Starship Traveller*, a bit of a limp attempt to bolt the format on to a piece of hard sci-fi. The two writers fairly soon farmed out the writing to others, still with their names on the cover as 'presenting' the stories. By the time the series came to an end in 1999, it contained over 70 titles.

RetroFax

- Another writer for the series was also, confusingly, called Steve Jackson – a Texan and the founder of Steve Jackson Games in the USA
- The series was intended to end with book no. 50, *Return to Firetop Mountain*. However, sales were so good that the series was continued for further 9 books and ended with no. 59. Book 60, *Bloodbones*, was scheduled but never released

- There was also a 'First Adventures' series for younger children
- The books continue to be popular and have been reprinted many times in different editions
- There are some recurring characters in the books, such as the demonic Balthus Dire, first introduced as an adversary in *The Citadel of Chaos*
- The books have adapted themselves for a new generation – versions are available on the Nintendo DS, for example (to mixed reviews)
- Steve Jackson (the original) eventually did create that how-to book, published as *Fighting Fantasy: The introductory Role-Playing Game* by Puffin in 1984. It was a very entertaining guide which gave you the lowdown on how to become a Gamesmaster, complete with a sample mini-adventure
- A Fighting Fantasy bestiary called *Out of the Pit* followed in 1985

Games Workshop
A British game production company founded in Nottingham in 1975, with an interest in 'progressive games'. It went from strength to strength in the 1980s and 1990s, opening an office in the USA, and also expanding into Europe and Australia. Recently the company has been trying to expand into attracting an older audience, while still maintaining its younger fanbase.

See also
http://www.fightingfantasycollector.co.uk for a collectors' site with a full archive of book covers.
http://www.ffproject.com for fan-written online books.
http://outspaced.fightingfantasy.org/PDFs/FF_Solution_Maps.pdf offers online maps for many of the Fighting Fantasy environments – which seems to take the fun out of it, really...
http://www.ddo.com to play *Dungeons and Dragons* online.

The Cabbage Patch Kids
The essential: Cutesy ugliness personified

Born: 1983

Current value: Available inexpensively – most second-hand Cabbage Patch dolls tend to be offered for between £2 and £5. The newer Play Along models can be sold for £10–£20 in good condition

There's nothing quite like a tabloid outrage for getting a toy a bit of kudos and some extra sales, and the Cabbage Patch Dolls, or 'Kids' as they were more accurately known, benefited from a bit of *Daily Mail* huffing and puffing in the early 1980s. Originally known as 'Little Folks', then 'Little People', the Kids were the creation of Lorena and Michael Holmes – although they claimed to originate from one Xavier Roberts, supposedly a ten-year-old boy who had 'discovered' the Kids by wandering into a magical valley (as you do).

The Cabbage Patch Kids were brought to the wider world by Schlaifer Nance and Company, whose president Roger Schlaifer came up with the name and all the design and packaging. The way they were marketed as a phenomenon and a 'must-have' is to be admired on one level, although it is still inexplicable that such essentially unloveable-looking creatures won the hearts of so many millions of children. Part of the appeal, one supposes, was that they gave the impression of not being mass-produced – each Kid was given its own 'adoption certificate' from the famous Babyland General Hospital, and parents had to 'adopt' the dolls, not merely 'buy' them. 'What was your Cabbage Patch Kid's name?' is one of those nostalgic questions which adults of a certain age still ask one another.

The big breakthrough year was 1983, when the dolls were presented at the International Toy Fair and began to be the subject of attention in the world's press.

RetroFax
- A somewhat bizarre side of the Cabbage Patch phenomenon is the Babyland General Hospital, a real place in Cleveland, Georgia, USA, which purports to be the 'birthing' centre for the Kids. It's an old healthcare clinic converted into a theme park. Tourists flock there to see new Cabbage Patch kids being 'born', and the Hospital has its own Intensive Care Unit. History does not report if any Siamese Cabbage Patch Kids have yet been born
- The first Cabbage Patch Kids went on sale in the USA in 1983 and three million were sold in the first year, rising to over 20 million by the end of 1984
- In 1992, the Cabbage Patch Kids became official mascots for the Atlanta Olympics
- And in 2008, the USA again attached the toys to a major event in its life, when all of the Presidential and Vice-Presidential candidates were given Cabbage Patch avatars
- Various urban legends have become attached to the dolls over the years. One is that Cabbage Patch Kids returned to the factory for repair are given a 'death certificate' – one can only imagine the tears before bedtime. Another is the rumour, perpetuated in the early 1980s, that the design of

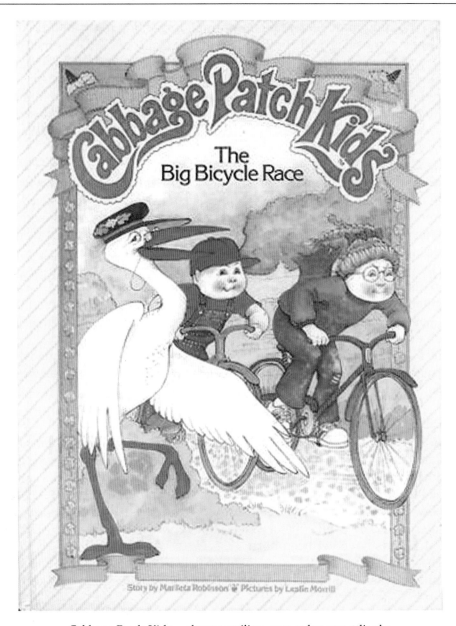

Cabbage Patch Kids – always smiling, somewhat unsettlingly.

the dolls was supposed to make them resemble strange post-nuclear-holocaust mutants – supposedly intentionally, at the behest of President Ronald Reagan. True, they lacked Barbie and Sindy's groomed Aryan prettiness, but this was taking things to extremes

- The Cabbage Patch Kids were voted one of *Time* magazine's 'Top 10 Toy Crazes' in an article from 2009

Cabbage Patch Doll with the usual air of smugness.

Cabbage Patch Dolls – they were 'born', you know ...

- Variants included porcelain versions and a 'Snacktime' model from the 1990s which, in somewhat sinister manner, could chomp on plastic snacks with moving jaws. This latter model was voluntarily withdrawn when it was found that it could easily attach to children's hair and pull clumps of it out, or that fingers could be caught in the mechanism
- Ugly parodies the Garbage Pail Kids turned up on a series of collectable cards in 1986

They Said What?
- 'They knocked over the display table. People were grabbing at each other, pushing and shoving. It got ugly.' New York store manager commenting on the near-riotous clamour for Cabbage Patch Dolls in *Time*, 1983
- 'My attitude to people who criticise it is that if they don't like it, it's too bad. I do tend to get the odd comment from people who ask, "How can you sleep with all those eyes staring at you?"...' Darren Knowlton, Essex coffee shop manager and collector extraordinaire of Cabbage Patch Kids, speaking in 1999 about his £30,000 stash of over 650 of the chubby terrors

He-Man (and the Masters of the Universe)

The essential: Muscle-bound, sword-wielding universe-saviour

First flew in: 1983

Main merchandise: Comics, videos and DVDs, costumes, toy action figures from Mattel

Current value: Varying hugely according to condition and collectability. Some individual figures, used, can be priced under £1. For others, such as a vintage collectable boxed figure of the warrior goddess character Teela, which is very sought-after and rare, collectors will pay £80 or more. Even the new figures from the 2000s series can be valuable if boxed and in mint condition – collectors will pay over £100 for a boxed, mint King Grayskull, for example. For other rare oddities, see below.

Just as offspring of the 1970s grow misty-eyed over *Bagpuss* and *The Clangers*, so do Thatcher's children shed a tear and allow themselves a snuffle for the passing years when they remember the inexplicably popular cartoon *He-Man and the Masters of the Universe*. The unimaginatively-named hero bestrode the airwaves in the 1980s, having evolved from his original comic-book incarnation, battling his arch-enemy Skeletor and guarding his true identity

Human, beast and robot – it's Man-E-Faces.

– Prince Adam. Yes, Prince Adam. Bit of a come-down, that. No wonder he gave himself such a macho alias. His green tiger, rather unfortunately called Cringer, transforms into Battle Cat at the touch of a bolt of energy from He-Man's sword. Fans will also recall *She-Ra, Princess of Power* – aka Princess Adora, who, in true mid-eighties *Dynasty* style, is revealed as Adam's long-lost twin sister.

He-Man eventually became a victim of its own success – as the market became flooded with other cartoon imitators, it struggled to survive. However, it was revived twice, first in *The New Adventures of He-Man* in 1990, then in a new *Masters of the Universe* series by the Cartoon Network in 2002.

RetroFax
* A live action film version features muscle-man Dolph Lundgren in the title role, and was a commercial flop
* Although He-Man is armed with a sword, he only uses violence as a last resort, preferring otherwise to outwit his enemies
* His famous battle cry was, 'By the power of Grayskull – I have the power!'
* He-Man's arch-enemy Skeletor was, according to the story, once a real man named Keldor
* Among of the most sought-after *Masters of the Universe* toys are the weird oddities the series sometimes threw up, such as Snout Spout, the fire-fighting elephant, Faker, the unconvincing android replica of He-Man, and Buzz-Off, He-Man's friendly bee comrade-at-arms. Vintage 1980s figures of these and other rare characters can be found priced at £12–£20

See also
www.he-man.org Fan community site full of resources.
http://he-man.us American fan and collecting site.
http://flyingmoose.org/heman/heman.htm A history of the character and the show.

They Said What?
* 'A blatant attempt to sell violence to children through the peddling of violent action toys... The brutal barbarian is still held up as a model. It's incompatible with the survival of a democratic society.' Dr Thomas Radecki of the National Coalition for Television Violence
* 'We're not writing over the head of our audience like some shows do, but the writers generally feel like they're being asked to write a more fleshed-out script. It's not dumbed down at all... Gaps have been filled in, connecting the dots as to who is this person and how does he relate to this situation and what's the motivation.' Bill Schultz, executive producer of the most recent *He-Man* series

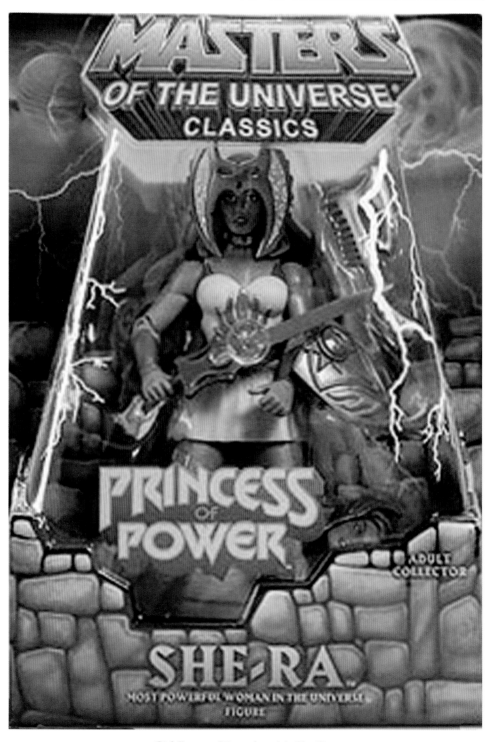

Girl Power, 80s style – it's She-Ra.

Superhero Round-Up

Just a few of the many collectables themed around the various multi-powered saviours of the world…

Superman: The Man of Steel has inspired collectable everything, from cheap lunchboxes at a few pounds to the rarest of action comics from the 1940s for which you would need to re-mortgage the house. Action figures which are rare-ish but may be affordable for the dedicated collector include DC

The extraordinary 'Bionic Bigfoot' figure from the *Six Million Dollar Man* range.

Direct's Cyborg Superman, worth around £120+, and the Hot Toys Clark Kent 2 in 1, for over £200.

Batman: A vintage 1960s Batman fashioned out of tin, made by Japanese company Tada, is a much-sought-after item and can attract a £3000+ price-tag. Apart from original film props, which always attract inflated prices, other collectables include 1940s DC comics (bagged) whose prices go into the hundreds of pounds, and a deluxe 13″ Joker figure, worth £180–£220 boxed and sealed.

Six Million Dollar Man: Aka Steve Austin, the slow-motion-running cyborg as portrayed by Lee Majors in the 1970s. Six million dollars not quite required, but at least £900 is needed to get hold of one of the rarest figures based on the series, a 1970s Kenner 'Bionic Bigfoot' (in its box), a creature with a disturbing resemblance to a cross between wrestler Giant Haystacks and rocker Lemmy from Motorhead. As for the bionic hero himself, one of the hardest figures to get hold of comes from the end of the range, when the programme and its sister show *The Bionic Woman* had been cancelled, and manufacturers Kenner were anxious to offload some stock by simply repackaging old figures in new clothes. Steve Austin in his orange 'test flight' suit, packaged as a 'Special Edition', could be worth over £300 on his own or £500 when sold together with the Bionic Woman 'Special Edition' in her green dress with blue belt and 'Mission Purse'.

The Incredible Hulk: A Corgi Mazda truck emblazoned with the logo and face of the green chap can attract around £60–£70. The 1970s Smash-Up Action Game from Ideal (sealed in its box) is pretty rare and can be worth £90–£100.

Wonder Woman: Quite reasonably priced in comparison to her super-hero colleagues, a DC Direct 'First Appearance' Wonder Woman figure, undamaged and unopened, can be found for £10–£15. One interesting oddity is a red-and-yellow Wonder Woman alarm clock from the 1970s, worth £15+ in good condition.

Thundercats: Based on the 1980s animated series following the adventures of a bunch of human/cat hybrids – they're due an imminent 2010s revival, which didn't happen on schedule. Among the most valuable items produced by Toy Options are the 1987 Ben-Gali with 'battle-matic' moving arm, worth over £1,200 (mint condition, boxed and sealed), and a Tygra worth £400–£600 (mint condition, boxed and sealed).

Tygra from *Thundercats*.

Transformers

The essential: Robots in disguise

First transformed: 1984

Current value: Hugely variable, and the range is enormous. Figures can sell for as little as £1–£2, up to over £80 for a sought-after item like a vintage G1 Defensor – and even more at auction for rare items (see below). The range also includes DVDs, T-shirts, voice-changers, gloves, chairs, holographic stickers... and far more besides

Perhaps the one toy, more than any other, which marks the mid-way point between the old-fashioned toys of the 1970s and the crazy, multi-media, marketed-to-death creations of today, where each character's place in the storyline is determined by how much revenue the franchise will be able to squeeze out of the collectable action figure. Hasbro's creations the Transformers always had as their key selling-point the fact that they could change, with a few deft flicks, from an ordinary vehicle into a battle-ready robot – which made them the ideal two-in-one toy, seemingly great value for money. The range has been through several generations, but the one most fondly remembered by nostalgic adults today will be the first phase from 1984–94.

RetroFax

- Hasbro bought up the rights to the Japanese Diaclone range, which featured robots able to turn into cars or weapons. The characters for the Transformers range were then developed by comic book writer Bob Budiansky
- The rarest Transformer figures are the G2 Protectobots, which are almost impossible to find and have gone for over £700 at auction

Transformers. They were, indeed, robots in disguise.

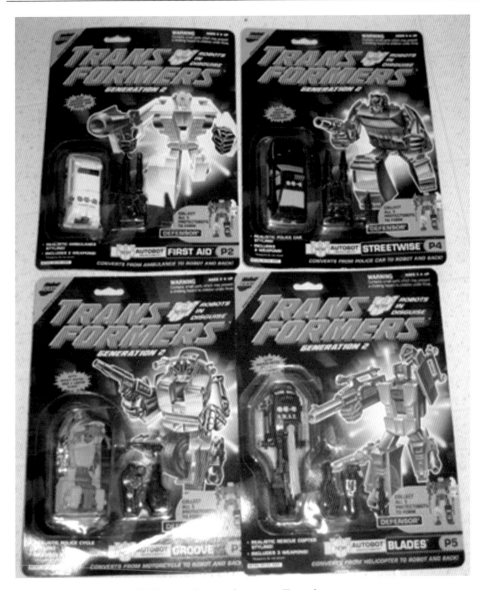

G2 Protectobots – the rarest Transformers.

- There's also a rather bizarre *Toy Story* range, in which the likes of Buzz Lightyear and Mr Potato Head appear to have molecularly fused with a Transformer

See also

www.ridforever.info is an extensive site devoted to Transformers lore. It features, among other things, an Ultimate Checklist of the franchise's characters.

The Sinclair C5

The essential: A revolution in personal travel – or maybe not

Trundled into view: 1985

Current value: £400–£500 in good working order

So, the famous Sir Clive Sinclair strikes again. Despite its rather comical appearance, the C5 was going to be the vehicle which transformed the way we get around. But it was a commercial disaster, mocked in the media, and only 12,000 were ever sold. In 2010, on the occasion of its 25th birthday, can we re-assess the C5 and decide that it was, perhaps, ahead of its time? After all, its ethos would seem to fit with today's green-anxious, low-carbon culture. It seems like the perfect vehicle for the twenty-first century anti-petrol-head. Launched in January 1985, the C5 cost £399 by mail-order – however, this had been slashed to below £150 by the autumn of 1985 when it was obvious it simply wasn't taking off. Despite this, C5 fans still speak enthusiastically of its futuristic styling, innovation and the way it embraced eco-technology.

RetroFax
- The C5 was injection-moulded, made of polypropylene
- Its battery was the 'deep-discharge' variety – unlike a car battery it is designed to be drained completely and then recharged. The C5 could do up to 20 miles before you had to recharge the battery

Sir Clive's C5 … it didn't revolutionise travel, sadly.

- Among the many C5 myths put about was that it contained a motor used in washing-machines. The C5 used a 12-volt DC motor, totally unlike the AC motor used in washing-machines. It's a fallacy still propagated by some websites today...
- The C5 had a top speed of 15 mph, with pedals for extra assistance on hills. This was the maximum speed an electric cycle was allowed to by law travel. And you didn't need a licence for it either
- The C5's launch did not go according to plan – it was held in the winter and the wheels skidded on the snow. The press vilification began, sales did not take off as expected and Sir Clive Sinclair lost about £8 million
- There were safety issues too. Wing mirrors, indicators and a horn, plus a high-visibility mast, were all sold as optional extras at additional cost – yet all were cited as essential items by the Royal Society for the Prevention of Accidents
- The technical website Cnet voted the C5 one of its 'Top 10 terrible tech products' of all time in 2007. Others included the Gizmondo hand-held games console, the Tamagotchi and the single-button Apple Puck Mouse
- Sir Clive went on to invent the Zike, a zero-emission motor for a bike with a price tag of £499 – also a flop
- In 2006, he unveiled the A-Bike (rumoured up until then to be called the C6), the world's smallest and lightest folding bicycle

---

They Said What?
- 'I would not want to drive a C5 in any traffic at all. My head was on a level with the top of a juggernaut's tyres, the exhaust fumes blasted into my face. Even with the minuscule front and rear lights on, I could not feel confident that a lorry driver so high above the ground would see me...' *Daily Telegraph* review, 11 January 1985
- 'If people change from cars to C5s that would be a positive gain for road safety in reducing the traffic load... but as an alternative to public transport there would be a problem, as there would be no change in the growth of car owners.' Geoff Large of RoSPA in 1985
- 'Sir Clive may seem an unlikely candidate for the Henry Ford of the 80s but if nobody ever took those risks, we would still be riding horses. There is a lot to praise in the C5, and many questions which only experience can answer in full. In the meantime, you have to admire his nerve.' *Sinclair User* magazine
- Sir Clive on the polypropylene body: 'Hit it with enormous force and it just bounces back.' Rather, it has to be said, like the eccentric British inventor himself

See also

www.sinclairc5.com Enthusiasts' site.

http://www.bbc.co.uk/electricdreams/1980s/sinclairc5 The nostalgia side.

www.c5alive.co.uk A site for enthusiasts which also sells clothing and gift
   items, plus spare parts!

Treasure Hunt Game

The essential: TV-inspired 'sky-running' shenanigans

Flew in by helicopter: 1989

Current value: Used editions are available extremely cheaply – sometimes
under £1

The TV show *Treasure Hunt*, made by Chatsworth Productions and shown
on Channel 4, ran for seven very successful seasons (1982–89), and made
a household name of the jumpsuited Anneka Rice. Anneka, flying around
the country in her helicopter, would be following the (often incoherent)
instructions of two erudite middle-class contestants who were based in the
TV studio with presenter Kenneth Kendall and had to work out a series of
five clues to the location of an ultimate treasure. It was all tremendously
exciting, and had to be achieved in a time-limit of 45 minutes. Anneka was
ultimately replaced by former tennis star Annabel Croft, who went on to
host the thematically similar (but more complex) *Interceptor*.

   The boxed board-game was made by Paul Lamond Games in 1989. How
much of the energy of the TV show it reproduces is debatable, but it is
well-made and captures the spirit of the programme. 'Location' cards and

The *Treasure Hunt* game ... jumpsuit, Anneka and Wincey Willis not included.

'Radio Message' cards guide the players around a map-board with the aim of visiting five different locations (as in the programme). The board-game doesn't reproduce the complexity of the TV show's clues, which were often fiendishly difficult and meant that the contestants required a bit of not-so-subtle prompting by Kendall.

RetroFax
- A computer game for the ZX Spectrum and Commodore 64 was also produced
- In 2002, the TV show was briefly revived, with Dermot Murnaghan as the presenter and Suzi Perry doing the tight-jumpsuited action stuff. It only lasted for a single one-week series.

Other board games based on TV shows
Some of the many board games inspired by TV game shows over the years include:
- **Countdown:** Channel 4's classic game-show, very easy to reproduce in box-form but without the banter and puns of Richard Whiteley. Repackaged several times over the years. 1980s editions in very good condition worth about £5

I'll have a P please, Bob.

Two from the top please, Carol.

- **Blankety-Blank:** BBC word-quiz with Terry Wogan was adapted into a board-game by MB games in 1983. There were subsequent DVD versions which perhaps recreated the atmosphere of the show a little better, but the 1980s board-game can be found at under £3
- **Blockbusters:** I'll have a P, Bob. Created by Waddingtons in 1986 and based on the popular game-show for teenagers – available cheaply, at under £2

And then, of course, we have the dozens of sci-fi-based board-games such as:

- **Masters of the Universe:** He-Man-based game adorned with a painting of the hero in the fray with Battle Cat, and designed for six players between the ages of five and 10. Based around the idea of retrieving lost treasure from Skeletor's base beneath Snake Mountain. There is a very rare 'pop up and play' game from 1982, as well, which can sell for over £40

Star Trek – one to boldly play.

- **Star Trek:** Various role-playing and board games based around the different incarnations of the Starship Enterprise. Among the most valuable are the Star Trek chess sets from the Franklin Mint, designed to be collectable and selling for £150+. The vintage Original Series board game and the 1992 Final Frontier game can be found for around £30. Live long and prosper
- **Battlestar Galactica:** Games based on both incarnations of the sci-fi western – the original 1970s game can be found for around £30

Gadget Decade: the 1980s

- Home computers became popular – largely as games machines, but also for budding programmers
- The LCD watch – Liquid Crystal Display – took over from the LED. For a while it seemed nobody would ever want an analogue watch again...
- Film blockbusters popular with eighties teenagers included the two *Star Wars* sequels, computerised fantasies like *WarGames* and *Electric Dreams*, and the emerging clutch of 'high school' movies like *Ferris Bueller's Day Off*, *Heathers* and *The Breakfast Club*
- Small-screen revolutions were the arrival of Channel 4 in 1982, followed by the dawn of Breakfast TV. *EastEnders* arrived on BBC1 for the first time, Michael Grade cancelled *Doctor Who*, and ITV's *Buck Rogers in the 25th Century*, *Robin of Sherwood* and *The A-Team* offered alternative fantasy worlds. Home video revolutionised how people viewed TV
- The Star Wars project and the proliferation of nuclear armaments sent shivers through the nation – especially those who had seen post-apocalypse dramas *Threads* and *The Day After*
- Early eighties electro-pop like Heaven 17, Soft Cell and Depeche Mode gave way to bombastic American rock like Europe and Starship, with George Michael, Madonna, U2 and Michael Jackson emerging as the biggest artists of the decade. As the eighties slid into the nineties, the influence of house and rave music began to be heard in records like *Pump Up The Volume* by MARRS
- Reporter Michael Buerk's account of a 'biblical famine' in Ethiopia led to an international fundraising campaign and the staging of Live Aid, the biggest charity concert ever seen

Chapter 4

Spice Up Your Life

Top Nineties Gadgets

- **Sega MegaDrive:** The sought-after games console of the decade, famously associated with Sonic the Hedgehog (who even had his own spin-off series of books). Called the Sega Genesis in North America. Obsolescence works against their 'retro' value now and they can often be found for under £10, although sometimes for as much as £40
- **Super Nintendo:** The rivalry between Sega and Nintendo has been well-documented… Super Nintendo consoles can change hands for a wide variety of prices depending on condition on the games thrown in with them, but £30+ is not uncommon

One for the 90s kids – the Megadrive.

The Psion organiser –
height of sophistication
in the early 1990s.

- **Tamagotchi:** the 'virtual pet' and its imitators such as PixelChix (see separate entry).
- **Satellite TV:** Sky in 1989, followed by BSB with its famous 'squarial' in 1990 – suddenly, the number of channels available was set to increase exponentially
- **Personal Digital Assistant:** the computerised nineties answer to the eighties Filofax – popular model was the Psion 3c
- **The Discman:** Sony's D-50 portable CD player was actually available in 1984, but as CDs caught on it was popularised throughout the 1990s. Varies hugely in price, from £10 for a used-condition model up to £40+ for one in good condition

Teenage Mutant Ninja (Hero) Turtles
The essential: Sewer-dwelling turtle fighters of evil

First flushed out crime: 1990 was the date of their peak in the UK (although the first animated TV series was in 1987, and the comic books date back to 1994)

Current value: Many collectables, including a very rare Turtles cookie jar, which has recently changed hands for approximately £415. The Turtle figures themselves are not horrendously over-priced for collectable items – a job-lot of all four can be found for £50–£60

The Teenage Mutant Ninja Turtles arrived in a blaze of publicity, bringing the usual attention-grabbing controversy that every new toy needs – the

Turtle Power!   The Ninja Turtles – sewer-dwelling heroes.

word 'Ninja' in the name, deemed to be too violent for the British market, had been replaced by the more innocuous 'Hero'. The foursome was made up of the easy-going, wisecracking Michaelangelo, the brlliant scientist Donatello, the bellicose Raphael and their leader, the experienced Leonardo. In the late 1980s, action figures began to flood the stores, with one London branch of Army and Navy even giving over an entire floor to Turtle-based shenanigans. They featured in their own TV series, a succession of films and several video games before gradually losing popularity in the 1990s.

RetroFax
- Just as The Simpsons and the Teletubbies would do later, the Turtles inspired a Number One hit single in the UK – *Turtle Power* by Partners in Kryme. The record knocked Elton John off the top and stayed there for four weeks
- Food ranges celebrating the reptilian reprobates were also popular – they had their own cereal available to buy, as well as Ninja Turtles Pudding Pies
- The TV series introduced the well-known catchphrases 'Cowabunga!' and 'Turtle Power!'

See also
www.ninjaturtles.com Official site – information on the toys, the animation and the movies.

Those Teenage Mutant Ninja (or Hero) Turtles got everywhere.

The Talkboy

The essential: Voice-manipulating cassette recorder

First spoke to us: 1993

Current value: The Talkboy can be found at under £2, while the rarer Talkgirl sells for around £5

As made infamous by Macaulay Culkin in *Home Alone 2: Lost in New York* – it's a variable speed tape recorder and player. Interestingly, rather than being a merchandise spin-off, the idea came first as a fictional one, just a prop in the film – but fans wrote letters demanding to know where they could get hold of the toy for real. So it was developed afterwards by Tiger Electronics. It's a handheld cassette recorder with a grip handle and a microphone, and as well as all the usual controls it has one for toggling between the different speeds. (We are amused by the idea of this consumer demand fuelling a commercial release of an item – imagine thousands of *Star Trek* fans clamouring for a real-life working Transporter or Holodeck, for example...)

The Talkboy – useful if you ever find yourself Home Alone.

The Talkgirl – for female Macauley Culkin fans.

RetroFax

- There was also a pink version called the Talkgirl – no gender stereotyping there, then...
- Other versions included the Talkboy/Talkgirl FX Plus, with additional sound effects, and the Deluxe model with a retractable microphone
- A similar, but cheaper and more compact device called the YakBak emerged in the late nineties.

They Said What?
'The allure of the toy, according to Roger Shiffman, executive vice president and co-founder of Tiger Electronics, is in the one-handed operation with a three-position switch (pause, slow speed, fast speed) that allows for recording in any combination of voice speeds, as well as its silver-gray high-tech look... The manufacturer said it is both ecstatic and frustrated – elated by the demand but unable to meet the overwhelming consumer response. It is fielding about 300 phone calls daily from consumers nationwide, eager to find out where they can buy a Talkboy, which retails for $29.99.' *New York Daily News*

Beanie Babies

The essential: Poseable stuffed toys

First hugged: 1993

Current value: From as low as £1 for some editions, up to £200 for a Rex the Dinosaur (rare)

Possibly the Care Bears of the nineties, these stuffed toys were seen as hugely collectible for a while. They were filled with plastic pellets, giving them a different feel from other stuffed animals on the market. Nine main 'identities' were created: Legs the Frog, Squealer the Pig, Spot the Dog, Flash the Dolphin, Splash the Whale, Chocolate the Moose, Patti the Platypus, Brownie the Bear and Punchers the Lobster.

RetroFax
- Special edition Beanies: Garcia the Bear from 1996, based on Jerry Garcia from the Grateful Dead, and a Princess Diana Beanie to mark her death in 1997
- A successful magazine based on the Beanies, entitled *Mary Beth's Bean Bag World*, ran from 1997 to 2001

Beanie Baby Jurgen, sporting the German flag.

Those Beanie Babies – as 90s as Chesney Hawkes. Here's Basilico, the Italian Beanie.

The mp3 Player

The essential: More music, even more masses

Download: 1996

Replaced: The Walkman and Discman

Price when new: $250 for the MPMan F10 in 1998; $399 for first generation iPod from 2001

Sound. We need it, we thrive on it, we communicate with it. When primitive man banged a couple of rocks together and liked the cracking, thumping sound they made, little did he know that, millennia later, he'd be responsible for Keith Moon and Roger Taylor. Even more frighteningly, he'd be responsible for the strange clattering noises which go on underneath The Prodigy and Tinchy Stryder. And the recording of sound goes right back to the ninth century Banû Mûsâ brothers, the Persian scholars who invented the first ever hydropowered organ. Ever since Marconi first started conducting experiments in his attic and worked out how to get his antenna correctly rigged up, we've been fascinated by the idea of sending sound over the airwaves, of sharing it, of getting it out there to as many people as possible in as pristine a form as we can.

The democratisation of three-minute bursts of music has proceeded apace in our millennium, with illegal copies of digital downloads now being available at the touch of a mouse, and an entire generation growing up no more intending to pay for the streaming of their music than they would ever pay for the water from their taps. Some musicians have met this challenge head-on – the band Radiohead were so keen for people to hear their last album

The iPod, on its way to making CDs redundant.

that they even allowed punters to pay as much or as little as they felt it was worth.

The music revolution will be downloaded. We have truly entered the next generation of listening. Many buyers who pondered the range of CD compilations available in HMV or Virgin back in the 1980s and 1990s and thought they could do a better job of picking the tracks now have the chance to do exactly that with 'pick'n'mix' downloads. You no longer have to buy an entire album, complete with dodgy ballast track swept up from the studio floor which should really only ever have been a B-side. Indeed, you can now track down your favourite artists' B-sides, make a compilation of them and give them a suitably arty-farty title before burning them on to a CD, or just filing them on your iPod and listening at leisure. The concept of the 'album', some argue, is disappearing rapidly.

It all began sooner than one might think. The mp3 format was patented in 1989. Back in 1996, a company called Audio Highway created the Listen Up audio player, a device for downloading digital music content – all music is now 'content' or 'product' – on to a portable player. This was followed by the MpMan from Saehan Information Systems based in South Korea, a 32Mb portable player marketed in North America in 1998, and the Creative Nomad 'portable jukebox' from Creative Technology. It took until 2001 before Apple unveiled the first generation of the iPod, capable of storing 1,000 songs and costing $399. A bit of pushy marketing and the promotion of its 'Click-Wheel' feature shoved it forward to become the market leader.

RetroFax
- Puerto Rican singer Ricky Martin, of *Livin' La Vida Loca* fame, was the first artist whose music was available as downloads direct to mobile phones
- Creative's Nomad was in fact a rebranded Samsung YP-D40, and was also available under Samsung's brand name of Yepp
- One major environmental concern hangs over the mp3 player – the fact that they contain toxic substances like lead, cadmium and mercury. The number of junked, obsolete players ending up in landfills could cause an ongoing problem...
- In 2008, 61% of adults between 18 and 29 years old owned an mp3 player

See also
Digital copyright and the consumer revolution: hands off my iPod by Matthew Rimmer (Edward Elgar Publishing, 2007)
http://mp3-players.toptenreviews.com/flash-drive/ for comparisons of the latest, most up-to-date mp3 players.

The 10 Rarest Video Games Ever

10. **Donkey Kong Competition Cartridge (SNES)**
    Worth approx. £600–£650
 9. **Nintendo World Championships Gray (NES)**
    Worth approx. £3,300
 8. **NTSC Stadium Events (NES)**
    Worth approx £800 (cartridge only) or £26,500 in sealed box
 7. **Blockbuster World Championships II (Sega Genesis)**
    Worth approx. £1,300
 6. **Uncharted 2: Fortune Hunter Edition (PS3)**
    Worth approx. £800
 5. **Air Raid (Atari 2600)**
    Worth approx. £1,850 (cartridge only) or £12,000 with game box
 4. **Nintendo World Championships Gold (NES)**
    Worth approx. £12,000
 3. **Kizuna Encounter (NeoGeo)**
    Worth approx. £400 (Japanese version) or £8,000 (PAL version)
 2. **1994 Powerfest Cartridge (SNES)**
    Worth approx. £13,200
 1. **Nintendo Campus Challenge (NES)**
    Worth approx. £13,300

Source: JJ Hendricks of JJ Games. Ranking based not just on current rarity and pricing but also on estimated future value according to rarity.

Tamagotchi

The essential: The no-mess pet

Hatched: 1996, and relaunched 2004

Current value: The most expensive to be found are the Digimon Tamagotchis, still boxed and in mint condition, which can sell for over £100. Even Tamagotchis from 2004, selling for around £15 for a set of four, are sometimes described as 'vintage' – 1990s versions are hard to find

Manufactured by Bandai in the 1990s, Tamagotchis caught the headlines for the usual reasons of mouth-foaming middle-class outrage. The idea behind the toy was a simple one. It was a 'virtual pet' – over a decade before 'social networking' and the acquisition of 'friends' you don't really know on Facebook... The small hand-held device 'contained' a digital pet to which you had to attend like a real pet – feed and water it, give it love and clean up after it. But the *Daily Mail* classes were having none of it –

apparently Tamagotchis addled our children's minds and caused disruption in classrooms.

Three buttons controlled the various activities one could undertake with the virtual pet – feeding it a snack, playing games with it, checking its happiness and so on. There was the facility to make friends with (and even

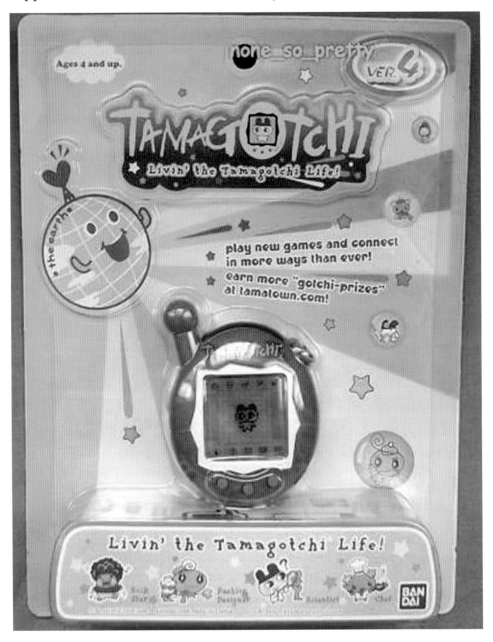

Feed that Tamagotchi!

marry) other Tamagotchis. Yes, in that brief period after the invention of the microchip and before the ubiquity of internet porn, it was the Tamagotchi which was briefly being blamed for the Downfall Of Society. Later versions included a convenient pause button. If only Real Life were so helpful.

The thinking behind the pet was that, by using simple commands in an effective way, children would learn how to 'train' it – praise, given effectively and early, combined with 'time out' punishments, would in theory result in good behaviour. This kind of thing tends to work well for small children, dogs and members of girl-bands, but was harder to get right with the little virtual critter.

RetroFax
- 'Tamagotchi' is a portmanteau word combining the Japanese word for 'egg' with the English word 'watch'
- The Tamagotchi was the brainchild of a Bandai employee, Aki Maita, who was searching for a 'perfect companion' to fit in with her busy lifestyle and small apartment, and which was also the right size for her to carry everywhere she went
- Forty-four different versions of the Tamagotchi have been released since 1996
- In the first wave of popularity in the 1990s, more than 40 million Tamagotchis were sold worldwide
- Tie-in films, anime TV series and songs have all been inspired by the toys
- The craze re-emerged in 2004 and Tamagotchis still sell well today, with a new generation of children discovering the joys of the virtual pets – which can now meet and play games through infra-red sensors
- This 'advanced Tamagotchi connection' enables a sort of Tamagotchi Facebook, where a list of up to 50 'friends' can be stored. They can even get married, have babies and disappear to Planet Tamagotchi, where they can be monitored online. (They don't, as yet, have the capacity to play Scrabble with one another, join fatuous-sounding groups or post Lady Gaga videos with small hearts beside them.)
- Other later competitors were FurReal (realistic fluffy pets) and PixelChix (digital girls inhabiting miniature digital houses, who can interact with one another when their little boxes are connected).

See also
http://www.ehow.com/how_2325375_choose-perfect-tamagotchi.html Tips on choosing the best model for you.
http://www.tamagotchieurope.com/ for the Tamagotchi Town.
http://3lib.ukonline.co.uk/tamagotchi/index.html Tips for parents – how to survive your child owning one.
http://www.tamatalk.com/ Community site – discussion forum for fans.

Teletubbies

The essential: Burbling, primary-coloured TV characters

First said hello: 1997

Current value: see below

Continuing the 'addling our children's minds' theme, the revolutionary characters for pre-schoolers, the *Teletubbies* (produced for the BBC by Ragdoll Productions) were the subject of a media storm in the late nineties. The particular focus of the ire of Middle Britain this time was not psychedelic references (although the Tubby Custard and the bright colours were a bit suspect, and it was no coincidence that the programme had a big fan-base among hungover students). Nor was it sexual references (but Tinky Winky's purple colour and triangular antenna didn't exactly endear him to some of the less gay-friendly parts of the USA, who read a message where there wasn't one).

   No, the problem was that the moon-faced Teletubbies didn't use correct English and behaviour for the young viewers to imitate. They dared to speak, move and act like giant, comical exaggerated toddlers. They burbled, giggled, fell over and generally enjoyed slapstick in their strange, ultrabright golf-course world with its trendy eco-home and robot vacuum cleaner, the NooNoo. They also sported TVs in their chests and, after watching a *Play School*-style film about children in action, would immediately clap their hands and demand 'Again, again!' Those who complained had, of course, spectacularly missed the point – and the programme spearheaded the BBC's love-bombing of the pre-school audience in the 2000s with its range of programmes on the new digital channel CBeebies.

RetroFax

- 365 episodes were produced between 1997 and 2001, giving the BBC an entire year's rotation of Tubby madness
- The Teletubbies' theme song, *Teletubbies say "Eh-oh!"* , was a Number One hit single in the UK in December 1997, just before Christmas. However, the festive chart-topper did still go to a brightly-coloured, child-friendly, larger-than-life bunch of repetitive gigglers, as the Tubbsters were knocked off the top by the song *Too Much*, performed by the Spice Girls.
- The sun beaming down on Teletubby-land bore the smiling face of baby girl Jessica Smith – and as her giggle is used on the record, this technically makes her, at under one year old at the time, the youngest person to perform on a Number One hit single!
- The (minimal) narration for the show was recorded, among others, by eighties pop-star and actress Toyah Willcox

Main Merchandise

The Teletubbies were a marketing man's dream. Soft-toy figures of varying sizes were made available representing each of the four Teletubbies: Dipsy (the green one), Tiny Winky (purple), Laa Laa (yellow) and Po (the red one, with the scooter). Talking toys appeared too. Also on offer was a huge range of the kind of items which doting parents of toddlers would buy for their Tubby-obsessed offspring: duvet covers, bath squirters and the like. Good quality Teletubby merchandise tends to be hard to find second-hand, as, by its very nature as a baby/toddler toy, it will probably have been chewed, pulled apart and dunked in water or other more unmentionable fluids. Somewhat disturbingly, perhaps, the Teletubby-related items commanding the highest price are adult-sized fancy dress costumes for each of the

Teletubbies games, for toddlers everywhere.

Tinky-Winky, darling of the American Right.

Vital to know your Teletubbies. Laa-Laa was the yellow one.

The Number One single featuring the youngest performer to date.

characters, which can fetch upwards of £200 each. We can only speculate as to why anybody would want one, and move swiftly on. A full set of four talking figures in sturdy plastic, in working order, is rare and can set you back £25–£30. But items such as the scooter, board books, set of games and play mats can be found literally for pennies if you are happy to put up with a bit of wear and tear. A copy of the seminal CD single – if you are a Number One completist or wish, for some other unfathomable reason, to subject yourself to it – can be found pretty easily for £1–£2.

They Said What?
- 'The combination of space twaddle, endless repetition, and toddler antics gives the show a kind of fey, otherworldly aura, but it's a mistake to dismiss *Teletubbies* as a weird, frivolous bit of entertainment. The program is extremely popular among both children and parents.' The Trouble With Teletubbies: The Commercialization of PBS By Susan Linn, EdD and Alvin F. Poussaint, MD, in *The American Prospect*, May/June 1999.
- 'They are babies… technological babies. Like children, they also imitate what they hear, so they will attempt to speak like the Narrator and sometimes like the Voice Trumpets.' Anne Wood, creator of the characters for the BBC. (The Voice Trumpets were the surreal, funnel-like public address systems which sometimes rose, periscope-like, from the Tubbyland grass.)

Furbys
The essential: interactive talking toy

Fur first flew: 1998

Current value: Generally under £5

For the parent of a small child in the late nineties, the Furby was disturbing. It seemed to have crossed the line; a hybrid of seventies fluffiness and new technology, as if your child's Teddy Ruxpin had suddenly been fitted with Terminator technology, or Bagpuss had somehow acquired interactive wetware. For those with teenage memories of seeing the film *Gremlins*, there was an equal layer of unease.

The Furby first appeared at the International Toy Fair of 1998, and started to fly off the shelves. It was the must-have toy of 1998. With its big, doe-like eyes, its bat-like ears, beak and strokeable fur, the Furby was an odd mixture of the cute and the grotesque, as if the spirit of the Care Bears had possessed something out of *Babylon 5*. It was even more unnerving thanks to its developmental capacities – it started out speaking its own language, Furbish, and gradually started 'learning' English (no matter where it was brought up – an opportunity missed there for Scottish Nationalist or Basque separatist Furbies).

RetroFax

- In 1999, the Furby was suggested as being a threat to national security. The Furby was banned from US National Security Agency premises thanks to fears that it might go home and start blabbing secrets. (And that was in more innocent pre-9/11 times. Two years later, they'd probably have been shot on sight.)
- Hasbro issued a 'Furby Care Guide', now available as a downloadable PDF. One of the instructions contained in it was 'Do Not Submerge In Water', and also 'Do Not Get Wet'. Any *Gremlins* fans who hadn't felt disturbed yet surely did by now
- A rare item is the 'E.T. Talking Furby' from 2000, which in good condition and in its box is worth around £30. The head extended and the finger lit up...

See also

http://www.langmaker.com/furbish.htm offers a guide to the Furbish language.

www.adoptafurby.com for all your Furby needs.

Furby. He's listening, you know.
Don't tell Mulder and Scully.

Gadget Decade: the 1990s

- The electronic age was well and truly here. Nineties children and teenagers, au fait with computers, entertained themselves with Tamagotchis, Nintendos and the SegaMegadrive
- Mobile phones, at first chunky and laughable and then sleeker and lighter, started to gain in popularity
- John Major was succeeded as Prime Minister by Tony Blair, whose landslide victory in May 1997 brought Labour to power for the first time in a generation. Across the pond, the Democrats were back in power with Bill Clinton
- The death of Princess Diana in 1997 resulted in nationwide mourning, with many people placing flowers in front of Kensington Palace
- Homegrown sci-fi went through something of a lull in the UK – with *Doctor Who* on a time-warped sabbatical, the most popular TV shows rooted in the weird and wonderful were US imports like *The X-Files*, *Babylon 5* and *Buffy The Vampire Slayer*. The most popular comedies were American imports too – *Friends*, *The Simpsons* and *Frasier*
- People began to talk about their 'electronic mail addresses', and this thing called 'dial-up internet' which would connect their computers to the rest of the world
- And they nervously discussed the Millennium Bug, which was supposedly going to make all computers crash and cause planes to fall out of the sky...
- In the charts, the heart of the decade was defined by the Britpop battle between Oasis and Blur. One side of that lay a flirtation with the grunge of Nirvana and Pearl Jam alongside the new British acts like Suede, Stereo MCs and Saint Etienne – while on the other, audiences experienced the growing influence of drum'n'bass rhythms and techno and the late-nineties proliferation of boy/girl bands...

Chapter 5

Some oddities and rarities

Very occasionally, the consumer world throws up something so bizarre that you wonder whether anyone actually bought it at the time, let how it has endured as a collectable... Here are eight of the strangest, most loveable or unloveable, forgotten or half-remembered, iconic and unedifying devices we may or may not have desired...

The Seiko Drum Machine Watch

The LED became the LCD, and then the calculator watch provided a new twist. But it wasn't over yet. In a 1990s variation on the digital watch, Seiko produced the rave-inspired 'Frequency', a drum machine in the form of a wristwatch with a distinctive yellow or silver casing. It can sell as a vintage item now for over £300. Much sought after by old ravers.

For ravers everywhere – the drum-machine watch.

The 'Allo 'Allo board game

We all remember David Croft's *Secret Army*-pastiche comedy run-around from the 1980s, in which the hapless René would attempt to hide British airmen from the Germans in ever-more-farcical situations involving Knockwurst and the painting of the 'Fallen Madonna with Ze Big Boobies'. Somewhat incredibly, the comedy series was turned into a themed board game in 1989. Players are either in the French Resistance, whose aim is to smuggle the British airmen over the border without being captured, or in the German army attempting to capture them. Yes, seriously. Listen very carefully, ah shall say zees only once: it's a rare item, and can change hands for £20 in good condition.

'You may be wondering what ah am doing in a board game.'

The TARDIS Rubik Cube

The perfect geek item, one might have thought – the Doctor's transcendentally-dimensional Police Box in the form of the mind-bending Rubik Cube. So rare that most Whovians aren't even aware it exists. Well, yes, that's because technically, this one is a bit of a cheat, and thus difficult to value – it's a fan's construction made by putting some printable TARDIS images on a customisable sheet of Rubik Cube Custom Sticker Kits...

Dimensionally transcendental – the TARDIS Rubik Cube.

The Calculator/Lighter

The Casio QL-10, to give its correct name. And yes, it really was a combination of cigarette lighter and calculator, which seems to take multi-tasking to absurd lengths. Now worth approx. £100–£110.

The Casio QL-10. Multi-tasking for the smoking mathematician.

Two-armed Davros

The fearsome Davros, creator of the Daleks in his electric wheelchair – whose wizened face and single claw-like hand had made so many children cower behind cushions in 1975 – was produced by Dapol as a figure with a rather splendid additional arm. The two-armed Davros was withdrawn in 1990, with a somewhat unapologetic comment from Dapol manager David Boyle: 'We're making a range of toys *based* on *Doctor Who*. If we wanted to

Davros, feared one-armed creator of the Daleks. Spot the problem here.

make fully detailed models, we could do that.' Um... The rarity value of a Davros fully able to do a bit of knitting means that he can change hands for around £60+.

Tetris Board Game

Tetris, the addictive, fast and furious shove-the-blocks-in the-holes video-game, depends for its fun and difficulty on quick thinking and increasing pace. Which of course is why it exists as a board game. No, really, it does. Players race against each other to slide plastic pieces into place in an attempt to reproduce the furious action of the on-screen incarnation. The effect is somewhat like moving a counter around a pencil-and-paper maze to pretend you are playing *Pac-Man*. Produced in 1989 by Tomy, it's supposedly worth up to £40... if you really want to.

Yes, there really is a Tetris board game.

Playmobil's Hazardous Materials Team

Now, you too can play at cleaning up after a serious toxic biological waste incident... Presumably they are sent in once the rest of the Playmobil population has been evacuated to a place of safety, like the sofa.

Playmobil Hazardous Material Team. Look, sometimes it's just best not to ask.

The C-3PO Tape Dispenser

A Japanese porcelain sellotape dispenser in the shape of friendly *Star Wars* Droid C-3PO, with the friendly robot sitting up as if sledging and the roll of tape jammed rather inelegantly between his legs. We are trying to imagine a scenario in the film where such a thing might have arisen – or even something vaguely like it – and are struggling to think of anything. Not even in *The Phantom Menace*. Incredibly, some collectors will ask £90–£100 for this.

Possibly the worst *Star Wars* idea ever. Yes, worse than Jar Jar Binks.

Gadget Decade: the 2000s

- This decade, two more big Labour election victories were followed in 2010 by UK's first hung parliament since 1974 and the subsequent Coalition Government. In the USA, President Barack Obama swept to power in 2008 on a tide of new hope
- On TV, meanwhile, 'Reality' took over – the big successes were housebound nightmare *Big Brother* and karaoke extravaganza *The X-Factor*
- The pop charts began to be dominated by winners of the 'reality' shows, from the first publicly 'manufactured' group Hear'Say to the mega-successful pop goddesses Girls Aloud (who spawned their own merchandising crazes, including fake eyelashes styled around each of the five girls)
- In 2000, the arrival of the Jabra Bluetooth earpiece made it look as if everyone was walking around talking to themselves
- Mobile phones transformed into the ubiquitous iPhone in 2007
- The Amazon Kindle e-reader attempted to transform the world's reading habits... with many of us still preferring the old-fashioned book
- Computers became sleeker and shinier, with the USB flash-drive replacing the floppy disk as the portable data medium and the iMac and iPad doing good business
- The dawn of XBox Live in 2002 took computer gaming to a whole new level... while the arrival of the Wii Remote in 2006 took virtual worlds into a new dimension where every kick, punch, swing and throw was replicated on screen, opening up a veritable Olympiad of living-room sports
- The BBC's *Doctor Who* returned in 2005 to enthral a new generation, and with it came endless new gifts, games and gadgets – everything from plastic figures and Cyber-lunchboxes to the handheld computer game and the remote-controlled Dalek. A downloadable interactive game from the BBC website was announced in spring 2010

Afterword

The Future

And so we come to the end of our museum of futures past. If this were a building, you'd now be in the gift-shop.

As objects rust, shrivel, fade and are binned, others step up to take their place. The C5 may be a joke, but what about those motorised scooters – will we be chuckling at them in twenty years' time? But hang on – we all thought the virtual pet or Tamagotchi was a passing fad, and yet, a decade on, schoolchildren still have the little bleeping friends. And the mobile phone, like Sophie Dahl, is now less voluptuous, no less beautiful, but still as popular.

Yes, the more things change, the more they stay the same. Scratched vinyl is replaced by cassette, and then by CD and mp3. The Walkman gives way to the iPod, while the download makes even the physical form of a recording an obsolete concept. The linear format of the videotape gives way to the interactive, pick-and-choose DVD. Where before we could only watch as the bits of information unfolded in order, we can now jump in and out at will and zoom into Easter Egg extras showing the lead actor having a crafty ciggie.

The world moves on, and as the decades pass, we will no doubt look back at the gadgets and games of the early 2000s with fondness – and a little wry amusement. In the world, perhaps, of the interactive downloadable holo-vision-cast, we will find the iPlayer and the plasma screen worthy of amused recollection. Perhaps the iPad will take its rightful place in a museum when, in thirty years' time, every surface of the home is a touch-sensitive, information-rich repository of interactive 'infotainment'. When octophonic soundscapes are available in our heads at the tweak of an earlobe, we will reflect on how quaint the digital download now seems. And maybe – just maybe – we will one day get those jet-packs. Over to you, Sir Clive…?

Index